Encounters With God

Encounters With God

FAMILY CHRISTIAN STORES

www.FamilyChristian.com

Published by Family Christian Stores, 5300 Patterson Avenue SE,
Grand Rapids, Michigan 49530.

ISBN 1-59391-028-2

1 2 3 4 5 6 7 8 9 10

CONTENTS

Give Her to Me...1
Brenda Kopsa

The Cardinal, the Potter, and the Lump 5
Susan Abernethy

He Gently Leads...9
Pamela A. Angell

My Favorite Homily 13
Jennifer Bornholm

Evan's Prayer...15
Marilyn Buessing

Gentle Voice...19
Linda Burns

Ring of Faith 21
Autumn Byers

You Finally Found Me 23
Tonya Byrd

Seeking God 25
M. L. Clock

The Shoes of a Hero's Wife 29
Andrea Cooper

Through God's Eyes...35
Irene Costilow

The Conch Shell...37
Connie Crider

Waiting at the Fence 41
Dean Crowe

Only by the Grace of God...45
Melia Dickinson

God's Provision in a Time of Unemployment...........................49
Beth Doucette

Shadows 51
Janet Dowty

Jesus Wept in My Place...55
Christine Dunaway

The God of Miracles..59
Darlene Eastes

A Crumb from the Master's Table..........................63
Allison Garner

An Unexpected Gift Wrapped in God's Grace 67
Kelly Gerken

Stepping into the Light...71
Mandy Harris

Angel at the Bus 75
Derek Hastings

An Appointment in the Air 77
Susanne Horn

God is So Good! 81
Tom Houck

Finding Comfort in an Uncomfortable Place 85
Kelly Kauffman

Sometimes God Wears Skin..................................89
Christine Kozlowski

I Am Free 91
Joseph A. Mantini

A Subtle Hint 93
Rick Martin

The Tale of the Missing Purse 99
Phil Nicholas

My Turkey Buzzards...103
Renee Ortiz

Truth in Our Crazy World 107
Amanda Denise Osberg

Telling God What to Do...109
Tina Patete

Arrested by God's Love 113
Penny Phagan

Walking through Sorrow 117
Cindy Pocapalia

I Come to the Waters 121
Kathy Ptaszek

Consider the Lillies 125
Kathy Ptaszek

Because Forever is a Long Time 129
Chris Quinn

Showers and Flowers 131
Pamela Randles

God's Precious Care......................................135
Cheri Roberts

Identity Crisis......................................139
Jennifer A. Roberts

The Bride's Victory......................................143
Susanne Scheppmann

Be Pretty 147
Lisa Schroeder

God's Helping Hand 151
David Schuitema

Resurrection Power! 153
Gwen Shannon

Thankful Heart......................................157
Candace Sorondo

Tiffany's Faith 159
Charles Stone

It Couldn't Be......................................163
Melissa Sutter

God Still Performs Miracles 167
Dana Turner

Scar Tissue Issues......................................171
Makisa Upton

Scar Face, the Lily 175
Susan Veach

To Know All of Him......................................179
Kay Walsh

This is the Day......................................183
Cathy Welsh-Hulin

Bestseller in Heaven 187
Russell Williams

The Little Red Wagon......................................189
Sharyn McDonald

God's Perfect Timing 193
Jennifer Bornholm

Dear Valued Guest,

For more than seventy years, Family Christians Stores has had the privilege of impacting lives for Christ as a ministry-minded business. It is our passion to offer you a wide selection of Christian products designed to strengthen the hearts, minds, and souls of believers and seekers from all ages and stages of life. The book you now hold in your hands is an extension of our mission. It is filled with personal accounts from our customers of how God's hands have touched their lives,, ordinary people with extraordinary stories.

In addition to this book, the over ten thousand different products available in our stores and through FamilyChristian.com website, provide faith-filled, Christ-centered support in your journey to know and live for Him. We have Bibles for everyone from children just learning to read, to serious students who want to discover every nuance of Greek and Hebrew. We offer accessories like Bible covers, highlighters, tabs, and more. We have books for women and men, singles and married couples, kids, tweens, teens, and adults. You'll find the very best music from pop to praise and worship to minister to your heart. From cards and framed art to kid's toys and videos, we have whatever you need to enrich and enhance your lifestyle at Family Christian Stores.

We're also sensitive to your desire to be a good steward of the resources God has given you. That's why we offer a price matching promise, exclusive Perks program, and great monthly deals on the latest, most popular books and music. Flip to the back of this book, and you'll find valuable coupons to save you even more!

Thank you for shopping Family Christian Stores and FamilyChristian.com. We appreciate your partnership in reaching families and communities with the gospel and grace of Jesus Christ. We ask that you pray for us as we seek to operate our company in a way that best fulfills the mission God has given us.

Answering the call to help strengthen
The hearts, minds & souls of our guests,

Dave Browne
President/CEO
Family Christian Stores

GIVE HER TO ME

Brenda Kopsa

It was yet another sleepless night in the hospital room with my once vibrant, happy, little two-year-old. Her petite body had already endured endless rounds of chemotherapy, and she was tired and worn out from all of the pokes from needles and tests. Mouth sores from the chemo had kept her awake most of the night, and we were both very tired. Cami had been diagnosed with one of the most deadly forms of Pediatric Cancers, fourth stage Neuroblastoma, just two months prior.

She was restless as I rocked her and rubbed her head where her beautiful blond curly hair once was. I had asked the nurse to give her some pain medication to help calm her. I talked to the nurse as she was making Cami's bed and was waiting for Cami to get some relief from her pain when suddenly she went completely limp. I looked down at her and she was turning blue. Every part of me knew that something was wrong, deadly wrong. I screamed to the nurse in the room that something was very wrong. Looking at Cami, I stood up, and laid her down on the bed. Her eyes were rolled back, and I could tell that she was not breathing anymore. The nurse told me to go get help. I ran out into the hall screaming, trying to get someone to help us. By the grace of God, the first person to hear my cries was the respiratory therapist.

A code blue blared in the overhead speakers. I couldn't believe what was happening to my baby. It seemed like a nightmare; I just wanted everything to stop.

My legs gave out on me, and I was on the hallway floor watching in horror as doctors and nurses ran into my daughter's room. Someone called for the chaplain. There was so much chaos going on all around me when I suddenly heard a calm voice in my head saying, "Give her to me."

I shouted out loud to God, "No! You can't have her!" I tried with all my might to push that voice away out of my head. Again and again, calmer each time, God repeated, "Give her to me."

"She is mine. You can't have her," I replied. My heart was breaking, and I wanted to go back into the room with my baby. I started to crawl back to the room; I knew my legs didn't have the strength to carry me, and I couldn't see because of the tears. The voice was still saying, "Give her to me."

I saw the chaplain rounding the corner, and I asked him to help me up and walk me into Cami's room. I knew what I had to do. I needed to see my girl and say goodbye to her. God gave me Cami, and I had no right to tell Him that He couldn't have her. I asked the chaplain to help me give her to God.

"Please help me. I don't know how to let her go," I said to him. Tears streamed down my face and my legs still would not hold me up. I clutched the chaplain with all of my might. I saw her, my precious little girl, lying on the bed, listless. She had just had a grand mall seizure.

With every bit of strength I had left in my body, I cried out to the Lord and said, "She is yours!" As soon as those words left my mouth, Cami's eyes popped open, looking for me. I knew at that moment that she was right where God had intended her to be, in the arms of her mommy. God wanted me to stop worrying, stop trying to run the whole show by myself, and to step aside so that He could take over and be in charge of our lives.

We had a rough two and a half years following this, but Cami had beaten all the odds, and she is now a healthy, charming, bright, five-year-old. Throughout all of Cami's treatments, which were mostly experimental, she has not had any adverse side effects, and continues to baffle the medical world with her success.

Thank you, Jesus, for healing Cami!

┌───────────────── AUTHOR BIO ─────────────────┐

Brenda Kopsa is blessed and honored that God picked
her to be the mother of her little miracle girl, Cami.
Their home church is the Vineyard Christian Fellowship,
which has stood by their side throughout all of their
many trials. Her greatest joy in life is sharing God's
love and grace with others through the healing
of her precious Cami.

└───┘

THE CARDINAL, THE POTTER, AND THE LUMP

Susan Abernethy

I had never seen a real, live cardinal until I moved to Texas. And I had no idea that this little bird would end up being an instrument of both frustration and incredible faith building.

Three years ago, a cardinal adopted our backyard. His domain perimeter took him around our house, tree by tree. His song was a combination of different sounds at varying speeds and *loud*. He began chirping before daybreak and was amazingly punctual on a twenty-minute cycle. During the school year he never bothered me, since my husband and I rose before daybreak, getting our boys off to school. Everyone in our family looks forward to summer's change from hectic school schedules to lazy, sleep-in mornings. It was during the summertime that the problem developed.

The first summer he woke me every day before dawn. I am a light sleeper, and once awake, that's usually it. I became resentful as each morning he invaded my dreams, disturbing my sleep. Many mornings I resigned myself to dragging out of bed shortly after he started, sparing myself much grief. Other mornings I would *really* want to sleep in, then it was a vicious cycle of waking and dozing. I was upset, but there was nothing I could do about it.

The second year the frustration level rose. Feeling silly, yet knowing that God cares about every detail, I started praying that He would remove the irritation. "Let him start singing later, or in another backyard," I'd pray. I didn't mind it later in the day, just not so early! The wake-up calls continued. There were a few mornings without him. I would thankfully think, God did it! But then he would return, which left me feeling foolish.

The third summer was the worst. Someone might wonder if I needed to get a life, worrying about such a minor problem in light of the bigger picture. I didn't let this consume my every waking moment, but I *was* getting angry. Angry that God would not answer this simple little prayer of mine. I would think, *Let's get this settled and move on to more important things, God.* The worst part was that I felt God didn't care, or was ignoring me.

Another issue was control. I had none. I couldn't reason with the bird. I couldn't climb the trees and shoo him away. We weren't going to move! Buying a shotgun was not realistic (although it was tempting in a kind of sick, you-really-need-help sort of way). Most of all, I felt I couldn't get God on my side. He wouldn't answer my prayers the way I wanted. It was a downward spiral of self-pity nagging me. I tried everything to endure this depressing way of waking up each morning.

Finally, it was THE morning. Every other time the bird chirped for twenty minutes, tops. He'd fly away, and although he came back, it was a relief for awhile! After lying wide-awake for an unprecedented forty-five minutes of constant, unstopping noise from Mr. Cardinal, I was fit to be tied. Why hadn't I just gotten up? Simple: it had become a test of wills. I pleaded with God. I tried to relax and ignore the bird. I did everything, then I got plain *mad*. I kept looking at the clock. Surely in the next five minutes he'd fly away. Ten, twenty, forty minutes went by. He'd *never* gone this long before. I was convinced he was glued to the branch!

Finally I got up and stomped into the living room. I wrote in my journal: *I will have no quiet time today because God chooses to torment me with that horrible, wretched little bird.*

I'm embarrassed to even acknowledge this now. I was furious. My journal continued: *I have asked Him repeatedly to relieve me of that incessant little creature, but He would much rather torment me beyond words.*

I went back to bed to just rest, thinking surely the bird was gone by now. I lay down, and as the cool sheets settled and the room became quiet, I realized he was still out there chirping and twittering away! I could not believe it. At that point, something happened. I felt as if a part of me snapped inside. I gave in. I admitted I was broken and defeated. More than ever I realized I had no control over *any* part of my life. God is not in His heaven waiting for *my* beck and call.

I could rage, plead, or beg but I was still only a lump of clay. God was the potter and *He* was in control. How I continually forget that this is proof of my puny little brain. I was so ashamed of myself for railing at the great I Am. He is the Creator. I am only the creation. How patient and forgiving He is. He could choose to wipe me off the face of the earth at any time, but doesn't. I was truly sorry. I prayed an apology to God for stepping outside my boundaries, losing my temper and my understanding of my position with Him.

The *instant*—not a few seconds or moments later—but the *instant* I apologized to Him in prayer, acknowledging that He was the potter and I was only the clay, it was silent. At that *moment*, the bird stopped. I remember lying there perfectly still. Every muscle was rigid as if paralyzed, my ears straining, waiting for him to start up again. *I had just been part of a miracle!* I started to explain it away as maybe a coincidence. God stopped me, not allowing me to ignore His hand so clearly in my life.

The next journal entry reflected the lesson I learned: *It was for me! The bird was for me. How angry I become when little things won't go my way. I'm ashamed of my anger and tempted to rip this page out to erase the selfish behavior I exhibited. I hate backsliding into such rage and lack of trust. I pray I never forget the details of that little bird. The awe and wonderment I felt knowing God had responded to my humble prayer the very moment I uttered it. I can't think of a time when I felt more directly connected to Him. I've never seen such a direct answer to prayer.*

I could hardly wait for the next morning, wondering what would happen. About 6:30 am, three little chirps. The first one startled me awake. I wondered if it was only the beginning, but that was it. Three short reminders to reinforce my lesson.

Since then, there have been days of early morning chirping, and days of none, but there has *never* been another 45 minute-plus marathon. When I hear him now, he reminds me of who I am, and how much God truly cares about every detail of my life. It took three years to get an answer to prayer that I could understand, but only after I had finally learned the proper way to pray. Then, wow, what an answer!

──────────── AUTHOR BIO ────────────
Susan Abernethy lives in Arlington, Texas. Married
24 years to Mark, they have two boys, Trevor and Kevin,
who bring them great joy. Her interests include writing,
drawing, cross-stitching and stained glass projects. She
is a Bible Study Fellowship leader and works with
women's ministries in her church.

HE GENTLY LEADS

Pamela A. Angell

I arrived at the meeting thirty minutes late. After settling my children in with the other kids downstairs, I quietly joined the group of women in the living room. As I sat in the circle, I noticed each of them had their Bibles open on their laps and daily planners close by.

Even though it was only a planning session for future Bible studies, I kicked myself for not remembering my Bible and scolded myself further for not organizing my life around a calendar. *What is wrong with me anyway? I'm a pastor's wife. I may not use a planner, but I should at least remember my Bible!*

As I sat nibbling on a brownie, I watched and listened. We went around in a circle and shared spiritual goals for the new year. My mind was whirling as I tried to think of a goal God revealed to me through supernatural means. None came to mind. I was still wondering if I had brought enough formula and animal crackers to see my children through the meeting without incident. Feelings of inadequacy trickled in, then grew to a swell that flooded me.

When it was my turn, all I could do was share what a struggle it is for me to meet with God each day outside of crises. "That's my goal," I said apologetically. "I just want to keep plugging away at my personal quiet time with the Lord." The women smiled and nodded.

Now it was out. The pastor's wife struggles with reading her Bible regularly. The pastor's wife does not make time for God. She has a weak spiritual life. She did not even bring her Bible. Surely these women were thinking all of this and more.

When the meeting was over, I gathered my children and headed home. Reflecting on my contribution, all I knew for sure was that I had eaten more brownies than anyone else. I was distraught over my lack of spiritual discipline compared to these other women. Driving home I prayed, "Please, Lord, bring a verse to mind to help me through this." Only a song from Sesame Street came to mind. Things were worse than I'd thought.

I tried to console myself by putting things into perspective. Although I'm a pastor's wife, I am not a spiritual super hero, a walking concordance, a woman who tap dances on water. I am a real person with real struggles. I am a woman who relies on grace moment by moment. I am a mother of six children.

However, the word "excuse" is not in God's vocabulary—six children or not. So, over the next several months, I tried to prioritize my time with the Lord, but it just didn't happen. God seemed silent.

Little by little, I began wondering where He was? *Does He love me? Can He forgive my misplaced priorities? If I really love Him, why is carving out time to be with Him so difficult? If He really loves me, shouldn't I be hearing from Him?* I agonized over these questions.
I even wondered if my salvation was at stake. I grew increasingly spiritually despondent. I found myself retreating from God. The Enemy was waging a war that I felt powerless to counter.

Not knowing whom to tell, I decided to keep the war within me a private one. Not even my husband knew about it. I made this choice because he was facing major changes at church.

Then one week our adult Sunday School teacher distributed an article at the end of class. I stuffed it into my purse and forgot about it. A few days later, I cleaned out my purse and found the article. It looked boring. It was written by a German Reformed pastor who died in 1868. But I decided to read it before throwing it away. As I read along, I actually enjoyed the article. It was well written and thought provoking.

Then it happened. Near the end of the article the words jumped out as if they were God's handwriting. His message was so clear it was virtually audible. There was no mistake! He was speaking directly to me! This is what God said through the writing of Friedrich W. Krummacher:

> "First, beware of despondency, by which we prepare a
> feast for Satan. Second, withdraw not from the presence
> of the Lord, as if his heart were closed against us. Third,

think not that it is necessary to make a fresh beginning
to a life of faith. When such a one is overtaken by a
fault, he has no need of an entirely new transformation,
but only need of cleansing. He must let his feet be
washed."

Satan had been gorging himself on my despondency and guilt,
steadily sapping me of my confidence in Christ to approach the
Father's throne of grace. But there was God, meeting *me* at my kitchen
table. I left the table and went to the living room floor where I lay face
down and sobbed. "Thank you, Lord, thank you," I cried.The haze of
hopelessness that was hounding me began to lift. God had used the
powerful and pertinent words of Friedrich W. Krummacher as a
rainbow of reassurance of all He had promised. How faithful He is.
How grateful I was. He took me in my quiet despair and gently led
me to a renewed awareness of the faith, hope, and love I have in Him.

Since that moving encounter with God, it has taken His
continued patience with me to make changes in my life. But like a hot
air balloon with its sandbags cut away, I am gradually rising to new
heights in Him. When a trip to Wal-Mart runs amuck, my children
echo His love and forgiveness as they throw their arms around me.
When a day at home feels more like a year, God grants me the grace
to let His omniscience and omnipotence reign, transforming drudgery
into ministry. Now my spiritual life is more than a quiet time. It is an
attitude of anticipation of what God is going to do in my life daily.

I still meet with that group of women, but things have changed. As I
sit among them, I continue to consider my walk with the Lord. Instead
of preparing a table for Satan, I feast on the Bread of Life, knowing He is
glad to feed me. Instead of retreating from God as a failure, I run to Him
as a prodigal, knowing He is waiting to hold me. Instead of allowing
spiritual droughts to parch me, I seek refreshment from the Living Water
of His Word, knowing He is able to quench me. Instead of doubting my
salvation, I claim His promises, knowing He is eager to have me live a
victorious life through Christ Jesus.

Being a full-time mother comes with many pressures and
distractions to be sure, but a verse from Isaiah reminds me that
God understands.

*"He tends His flock like a shepherd: He gathers the lambs in His arms and carries them close to His heart; **he gently leads those that have young.**"* (Isaiah 40:11, NIV) Today, I thank God for leading me gently.

─────────── AUTHOR BIO ───────────
Pamela Angell is a pastor's wife and a mother of six
children. She home-schools and co-leads a young
mom's Bible study at her church.

MY FAVORITE HOMILY

Jennifer Bornholm

"If we confess our sins, he is faithful and just and will forgive us our sins and purify us from all unrighteousness." (I John 1:9, NIV)

I sat in the rigid wooden chair waiting for my turn. I was next. The light was still red, and I sat there hoping it would stay red. When it turned green, it meant that it was my turn and I would have to go inside. As each second passed, my palms got sweatier and my heart beat faster. I had just committed a sin that I told myself I would never commit. I was sixteen, alone, and scared. So many questions ran through my mind. *What if my mom found out? What would she say? What would she do?* When I told the priest, would he kick me out and excommunicate me from the church?

Just then the door to the confessional opened and the light switched from red to green. My turn. I got up and slowly walked what seemed like a mile to the confessional. The small room was dimly lit with a lone light bulb shining from the ceiling. As I crept in, I saw the somber profile of the priest through the mesh screen. My stomach began doing summersaults and back flips as I trudged toward the padded bar I was to kneel on. And then I began.

"Bless me Father for I have sinned. It has been five months since my last confession." As I told my story of failure, disappointment, and guilt, the tears came streaming out. I could hold them in no longer. I had not only let myself down but I had also let Jesus down. *How could he love me now?* When I finished with my confession, I said the Act of Contrition and received my penance. I walked out of the confessional toward the back-most pew to say the prayers needed to gain the forgiveness I so desperately desired.

When I finished my prayers, I didn't feel forgiven. I still felt stained by my sin. As I got up to leave, I noticed the church had filled up. I looked at my watch and realized that the Saturday evening mass was about to begin, so I decided to stay. As the mass began, I felt too dejected to sing. As the lectors took their turns in front of the microphone to read their assigned verses, all I could think about was how God couldn't forgive me for my sin; it was just too awful.

When the priest stood up to give the homily, something made me stop and listen. His homily was about how God forgives you when you confess your sins! I couldn't believe it. God knew the guilt I felt in my heart and wanted to free me of it so I could worship and praise him. As soon as I heard that, it felt like a huge boulder was removed from my chest. Right then, I thanked God for knowing that I needed to be reassured of his forgiveness and meeting that need. God is so awesome! I spent the rest of that night and continue to live my life praising and thanking my God for the gift of forgiveness. I now know that I don't need to go to a priest to gain forgiveness. I can go to the Savior himself. And, based on scripture, I know that when I do, I will most assuredly be forgiven.

─────────────── AUTHOR BIO ───────────────

Jennifer Bornholm is an elementary school teacher in Orlando, Florida. She is an active member of Journey Christian Church. She is also an active member of the Chrysalis and Emmaus communities. Her hobbies include cross-stitching, reading, working out, and spending time with family and friends.

EVAN'S PRAYER

Marilyn Buessing

It is a bright Sunday morning in early spring. The air is fresh, the snow has melted, but my mood is dark and heavy. I keep thinking about family problems. I'm tired, not sleeping well. God seems far away. I'm driving to church to help teach the 4-year-old Sunday school class. I don't feel like going. I don't even feel very nice. But it's the last regular day of Sunday school.

I'm glad I'll be off for the summer. I need a break. I usually love being with these kids. I enjoy just hearing them say, "Hi Mrs. Jacobson!" But today I'm pushing myself just to get there. I'm unprepared and feeling guilty about that, too.

I pray as I drive, "Lord, I'm ashamed to say, but I'm not well prepared today. I really don't feel like teaching. I'm tired, I'm crabby, I can't think straight. I certainly don't feel godly this morning. Please help me be nice to the kids. Send your love for them because I'm empty. I don't have any energy to give them. Help me to at least be kind. And God, what do you think of me going home right after the class and resting on the couch instead of going to the worship service? I'm so tired! I need to recharge. Let me know what you think. Amen."

Class time went by slowly. I was grateful that my co-teacher, Mrs. Schmidt, picked up the slack. The children chose to sit on chairs, instead of the floor, at story time, and there wasn't *too* much fighting over who got to sit on the two coveted *blue* chairs. They sat in a semi circle in front of Mrs. Schmidt and myself.

With relief, I finished telling the Bible story. Then I said in my preschool teacher voice, "Children, today is our very last day together. Next week a different teacher, a *summer* Sunday school teacher will be here, and you'll have lots of fun!"

I had asked Mrs. Schmidt to pray after the story, so I turned to the her and continued with strained enthusiasm, "Let's pray, and thank God for the springtime, and the beautiful weather, the flowers and for each child in our class. Let's pray that they'll have a safe and fun summer."

I closed my eyes and bowed my head with relief. But before Mrs. Schmidt could draw breath to begin, I heard a tiny muffled voice say, "Dear Jesus." I opened my eyes.

It was Evan. His voice was muffled because he had bowed his head right into his lap so that his head was between his bony little boy knees. He was wearing shorts for the first time this year. He looked so small. I couldn't see his face, only the top of his head and his blond hair that was sticking up. I remembered that Jesus said to let the little children come to me. I was struck by the sight of a small boy easily and comfortably coming before the God of the universe.

I felt God's loving presence fill the room and encourage my heart. I kept my eyes open; I was glad I'd come today.

Evan continued praying, his voice going up and down, "And THANK YOU God for the SUN, and the BLUE SKY, and THANK YOU for the FLOWERS and..." His head was still resting on his knees but he turned to the side so he could see the child on his left. "And thank you for ABBY, and, and..." He looked at the next little girl in the row. He twisted his head even more to look up at me, his eyes almost upside down. Evan whispered loudly to me, *"I can't remember her name."*

"It's Ellie," I whispered back. He thanked God for Ellie and every single child in the class. He finished with a gracious, "And THANK YOU for Mrs. JACOBSON, and Mrs. SCHMIDT...amen." My heart was full. I felt loved, encouraged and thankful. God had used a child to bless me.

I stayed for the worship service.

AUTHOR BIO

Marilyn Buessing lives in Maplewood, Minnesota with her husband, Jon, and their 16-year-old daughter. They have a 23-year-old son, an older married daughter, Stacey, and a beautiful new grandson, Caiden. Marilyn teaches Sunday school and helps out with summer Bible school at her church. She enjoys listening to children, reading, writing, and looking for agates.

GENTLE VOICE

Linda Burns

On the last day of my ministry trip with International School Project to Ternopil, Ukraine in 1995, I was returning to my hotel room and entered an elevator with my dear Russian friend, Ludmila. My heart had quickly become entwined with these precious people, and I dreaded the good-byes, which were soon to come. As the old elevator labored its way up the floors, suddenly a gentle voice spoke saying, "Ask Ludmila if there is anything you have that she has need of." My heart thumped as I looked up at the elevator floor number and realized that within only a matter of seconds, we would reach our floor and part in separate ways. There was no time to think. Timidly, I repeated the question to Ludmila, and immediately I saw in her eyes that there was something. Fear struck my heart. What would she ask for? How precious would the price be?

We walked in silence to my hotel room. Ludmila sat down and cautiously eyed me. Sensing she was safe, she spoke in broken English, "Life isn't like it used to be back in Russia. We no longer live in the government palace or interpret for the Premier since we proclaimed our faith in Christ. Our home...it's not so nice now...we worry about disease and sickness. I noticed that you had a can of Lysol Spray. Oh please, if it's not asking too much, could I have it?"

Tears began to fill my eyes. Of all the things she could have asked for, this lady who had once held a high position in her formerly Communist country now asked for a simple can of Lysol as if it were a great treasure.

Oh God, forgive my selfishness and cleanse my heart, I silently prayed, now ready to hold back nothing.

Ludmila and her husband had sacrificed all their earthly possessions, security, and comfort to enable the gospel to reach their people, and here I was, afraid of what obeying the prompting of the Holy Spirit might cost me. "Is there anything else?" I asked. Again, timidly, Ludmila replied, "The needle and thread. I saw you sewing with such a fine needle and thread. They are hard to find. It would help so much. I no longer buy new clothes, but mend what I have."

Oh Lord! So it was you who spoke in the elevator! I was unaware of the needs of my dear sister in Christ, but God knew her every thought.

That evening as Ludmila and her husband drove off, their trunk was filled with all the provisions that it could hold. Though the road ahead would be perilous, I knew God's angels would go before them on their journey.

AUTHOR BIO

Linda Burns has had the privilege of being commissioned by the Lord to minister in Ukraine with International School Project. She is a wife, mother and public school teacher with a passion to be used by God, as his servant. As a young girl, she sensed that someday she would go to Eastern Europe to share the love of God. The day came when God wondrously provided, and this "divine destiny" became reality. Linda currently resides in Whittier, California with her awesome husband, Steve, and children, Bethany and David.

Ring Of Faith

Autumn Byers

When I was in fourth grade, my teacher asked the class to write a story about our most treasured gift in our house. It went something like this.

"My most treasured gift is my mom's sweet sixteen ring, which will be mine when I turn sixteen. The ring has a little purple amethyst in it with a piece missing. That is because when my mom was a teenager, a car hit her on her bike and she was wearing the ring. As she slid on the gravel, which tore up her leg, apiece chipped off. My mom lost a lot of blood and would have died if a man had not donated some of his.

"When my mom told me that story, she asked if I wanted the stone fixed when I turned sixteen. I kept telling her no, but would not give her my reason. Therefore, she did not understand and kept insisting that she have it repaired.

"The reason I did not want the ring fixed is because it reminded me of God's love, and that he was always watching over me. As my mom was lying in a ditch on the verge of death, He never left her side. That broken amethyst reminds me that He will never leave my side either."

After my teacher had graded the essays, I printed it out on a purple sheet of paper and took it home to my mom. When I showed my mom the essay, she began to cry. I watched her write something on my paper and then later on that day she handed it to my Grandma who lived a few minutes away.

One day while my grandparents were babysitting me, I started searching through their house for something to play with. I was extremely bored, so I looked through the desk in the playroom. As my hand fumbled around in the desk, my eyes caught sight of a purple paper. I slowly picked it up and unfolded it. On that sheet of paper was my essay. I reread it, and when I got to the bottom I saw my mom's handwriting. My mom had written: "Autumn wrote this story in school. I can't believe a child so young could have so much more faith than most adults. I am so proud of her. Please make a copy of this for me so I can have one."

A smile spread across my face as I read over and over what my mom had written. I'm not sure if what mom said was accurate. Only God knows how much faith people have, and I might not have more than most Christian adults. I just know that my God loves me more than I can imagine, and He will never leave my side.

─── AUTHOR BIO ───

Autumn Byers attends Leesville Road Middle School. She is thirteen and in the 7th grade. She likes to read, swim, play basketball, and listen to KLOVE radio station. She is a member of Capital City Christian Church and is involved in the youth group.

YOU FINALLY FOUND ME

Tonya Byrd

As I drove around town with my five-month-old son in the back seat opposite of mine, I softly called his name. "Gracson. Gracson. Here I am, Gracson." As usual, Gracson stretched his tiny neck all around as he searched for the source of my voice. He never discovered me, even though I was only inches away.

And then one day in the bank drive-thru, I turned to look at Gracson: he was looking straight at me! I exclaimed, "You finally found me!" He gave me a big smile as tears welled up in his eyes. He was so happy to know that I was there, even though I was there all the time. He was so happy, I cried. I will never forget the day when Gracson finally found me!

Instantly, I realized that's how God must feel. He calls out the names of lost souls, one by one. They search and search in all the wrong places. Until one day, they fix their eyes upon Him! They never realized He was there all the time. Tears must fill His eyes as He replies, "You finally found me!"

──────── AUTHOR BIO ────────
Tonya Byrd is a wife and mother of Ashlee (12),
Logan (10), and Gracson (3).

SEEKING GOD

M.L. Clock

Wednesday, April 24, 2002 was a day of contrasts. The morning dawned bright, but by evening, a thunderstorm raged across the Ohio valley. This divergent weather revealed, in a small way, how drastically things can change in just twenty-four hours. That single day brought the worst heartbreak of my thirty-eight years, and an encounter with God. One that made me look at the phrase *seeking* God in a whole new way.

In the last days of my father's life, I saw a living example of what it means for a man to daily seek and find God.

Dad was diagnosed with an incurable brain tumor in January of 2002. This news struck our family like a thunderbolt from a clear, blue sky! Our family, already close-knit, drew together like never before.

For as long as I can remember, Dad was a kind, godly man. But as his health rapidly declined, I witnessed him draw even closer to the Lord. Dad carried his Bible whenever he left the house, whether going to the doctor's office or just out for a picnic lunch. I cannot express how thankful I am for the comfort God's Word provided my father during his last, most trying days. Eventually, the sickness stole even the names of Dad's loved ones from his memory. Yet, miraculously, he continued to recite a favorite prayer over every meal. Countless times, during his three-month battle with his illness, I heard Dad utter the words, "God bless."

My siblings and I gathered at his bedside and held Dad's hand that stormy April night, as his treasured soul slipped from the broken clay jar of his body. This man, who had lived seeking the Lord, now needed to seek no more. I will never forget the last words my father spoke as he left this world behind. Barely whispered over the thunder outside, he said "Amen." A fitting end for such a prayerful, godly man.

Over the next few hours, my family gathered at Mom's side, comforted by one another's presence. Late than night, I left to drive home to my own family, little suspecting that God was about to perform a miracle which I will carry in my heart forever.

The thunder and lightning had abated, but the rain still poured. As I drove, I remember turning off the car's radio so I could pray. As I began to seek God through prayer, I felt strangely empty; I could form no words of prayer. Immediately, I felt an impulse to turn the radio back on, that God wanted to speak to me through it. This scared me! I've been a Christian for several years, and during that time, I've encountered God through small miracles. But never before had I felt such intimacy with the Lord.

My heart pounded as I switched on that radio. It was tuned to my favorite local Christian station, but surprisingly, the message God had for me that night would not be found there. I knew, as clearly as if the Spirit had whispered the words in my ear, what I had to do. I reached out and pushed the seek button.

Again and again, by the Spirit's prompting, I hit that button. The call numbers flashed by, but I was paying them no heed. I was listening intently, seeking the message I knew God had for me. The radio cycled nearly through the entire dial. Finally, it stopped on an oldies station, and I dropped my hand. *Now, listen*, the Spirit said to my heart. A song had just started, an instrumental from the Big Band era. As the haunting, scratchy notes flowed from the speakers, I realized that the music, though before my time, was familiar to me. When it fully hit me, I had to pull over to the side of the road. The song was *In the Mood* by the Glen Miller Orchestra. During their fifty-two-year marriage, *In the Mood* was what Mom and Dad had always called their song. Once my tears stopped flowing and I could drive again, I raced home. I had to call Mom and tell her.

With a song played over a car radio on a tragic, stormy night, a connection was made. God and I, through seeking, had found one another in a way that defies the ordinary. Through a song from a bygone age, God spoke words of comfort and promise straight to my soul. And because I was seeking, I found and was able to pass this comfort on to others in my family who were grieving Dad's passing.

AUTHOR BIO

Martin Clock lives in Goshen, Ohio with wife Patricia and their sons, Nick, Chris, and Josh. He's active in his church and co-leads a weekly Bible study group. He enjoys reading, writing, outdoor activities with his family, and seeking God daily through prayer and study of His Word.

THE SHOES OF A HERO'S WIFE

Andrea Cooper

My hope is that those who read this may gain a better
understanding as to what it is like to be part of the military. I do
not think that I need any kind of an award or even a pat on the back.
And I honestly do not believe that I am of more worth or any more
special than other women are. Truth be told, for now, this is my life,
and I only desire for my loved ones to understand the things that
I find so precious and hold close to my heart.

In all honesty, I envy the women who get to spend every night
sleeping under the same roof as their husband. I wish more than
anything that my husband had the freedom to choose his job and earn
the money that he justly deserves. I hate living so far away from my
family and spending so much time alone. In the past year and a half,
I have cried more tears of heartache than I have ever cried before.

At the beginning of the year, I spent nearly every day in absolute
fear that our president would call my husband off to war. But the day
came when my husband walked into the house, and when I saw the
expression on his face, I knew he was leaving, and very quickly.
I spent that night crying until my eyes were swollen and red. Yet
by the time we crawled into bed, we had reassured each other that
everything would be fine and that he would be back soon.

There were no tears when we hugged goodbye. He stood there in
all his gear and a half grin on his face. Pride swelled my heart. There
were not many words spoken. Too many would have caused the dam
to break and we would have never been able to control the tears.

The moment I drove off, fear like none other that I had ever
known wrapped so tightly around my heart that I didn't know what
to do. I had never experienced a war, and I had no idea what to
expect. I thought of all the possibilities and what I would do if my
husband were killed. I imagined the most horrific scenarios: scud

missiles dropping on the men's tents, atomic bombs that Saddam had hidden suddenly being dropped, and surprise attacks on my husband's camp. This went on for days until I finally got my first email from him.

I had decided from the start that the only way I would be able to get through the next few months was to keep myself as busy as possible. I wanted to support the Marines by doing all that I could do for their wives and by making sure that the families knew that someone cared for them. I had no idea at the time that this would become a unique ministry.

On Friday nights, I opened my house for the wives to come and work on memory quilts. Of course we never got close to finishing the quilts. We spent too much time eating and talking and at times venting all of our frustrations. We would watch Fox News, anticipating Oliver North's report on our Marines. Before the war, we would watch with wide eyes, hoping beyond hope that we would catch a glimpse of a familiar face.

I soon found that every woman who came to my house on Friday was also sitting beside me on the church pew. We would all hold hands when they sang God bless America. When one of us couldn't hold back the tears, another would put her arm around her shoulders and whisper that everything would be okay.

The day that the war began, we were all on the phone together making sure that the other was watching the news. We watched as the first bombs were dropped and marveled in awe at the fact that our men were part of this. They were fighting in a war! I remember leaping up off the floor and jumping up and down. I can't imagine that anyone else in America was cheering as the war began, but there I was jumping and screaming like a fool. The surreal part was that everything was happening live before our eyes.

That night all my excitement came screeching to a stop when Oliver North appeared on the TV for his report. Air Raid sirens began to sound, and Ollie announced that there were Iraqi missiles inbound. Before my husband had left, we had watched a special report on Operation Desert Storm. After having seen that special, I was scared at the thought of Iraqi scud missiles. I had looked my husband square in the eye and told him that I would be just fine as long as there were no missiles coming at him. Now here I was watching as our Marines ran behind Oliver North, pulling on full MOP Gear and heading for the bunkers. Needless to say, I was back on the phone with the wives.

The next day, we sat on my couch drinking coffee and watching the war unfold. Our fears quickly began to fade away as we watched our progress. Bombs rained down on Iraq and it seemed that there would be no way for the Iraqis to fight back. It appeared that they should be running away in fear and surrendering. Who would possibly fight back against such an overwhelming military attack?

Then that night the first American fatalities were reported. The nightmare was that those deaths were Marines from our squadron. At 6:00 pm on March 20, 2003, a CH-46 Sea Knight Helicopter crashed near the Iraqi-Kuwaiti boarder killing the crew and eight British Royal Marines. My phone began ringing non-stop as wives found out about the crash. They were panicked and wanted to know if their husband was okay. As their Key Volunteer, I told them that, as of yet, I did not have any information and would let them know as soon as I got the call. It was hard to hear women, whom I cared so much about, hysterical with overwhelming fear. I trembled the whole time that I held the phone to my ear and told them that we had to stay calm. By the time the calls stopped, tears had soaked the front of my shirt, and my heart pounded in my chest. *Was my husband okay?*

We waited in front of the TV and watched the ticker crawl across the bottom of the TV screen. All we saw for hours was "CH-46 Sea Knight Helicopter crashes, killing crew and eight British Royal Marines." Never in my life have I known the fear I felt as I waited for what seemed to be an eternity. I don't know how many times I held my breath as Oliver North appeared with a report.

Around eleven o'clock that night my phone finally rang and I was told that it had been confirmed that the helicopter that had crashed was indeed one of our own. I was also told that we had still not received information about who was onboard and that we would have to wait for yet another call when the information came in. The next few hours were spent thinking of the names of our men and wondering which ones might be dead. I wondered about where my husband was and what he was thinking. I cried when I thought of the heartache they were suffering, knowing that four of their brothers had been killed.

It wasn't until early in the morning that the phone rang again. The first thing that I was told was that my husband was alive and that all the ladies on my call tree were in the clear as well. I was to call the wives who were under my care and let them know that their husbands were safe and that notification of next to kin was underway. Until then we would not know the names of the Marines killed. We found out the names later that morning and the nightmare quickly became a reality.

I spent the next 24 hours making ribbons and banners in support of the troops. I cooked a meal for one of the ladies who had lost her loved one. I bought a card for our Commanding Officer's wife, whom I knew would greatly need the support after such a painful night of informing loved ones of their loss. I offered my services in any way I could as we prepared for a memorial service. Then I made sure that the women knew that the house was still open that Friday night to whomever wanted to come.

Our squadron suffered as a whole. Our Marines held their own service to remember their brothers. The wives stood holding each other up at the service held here at home. I have never really valued the sound of taps before the mishap. But this time, it was all I could do not to fall to my knees when the bugler played the ghostly notes and the CH-46 helicopters flew over in missing man formation. The experience was surreal and one that I never in my life would have thought I would have gone through.

For weeks it seemed that the memorial services would never end. The war had not been as easy as the country had thought. However, there was only one other time that the wives of our squadron had held their breath waiting to know if we had yet again lost Marines. In the end, the news was bittersweet. The helicopter that had crashed belonged to our neighboring squadron. Just the same, the men that were killed were Marines, and because of that, our hearts broke right along with theirs.

So why do I want you to know this and understand? Because I have experienced things that have changed my life forever. Through the tears, overwhelming fear, and heartache I have become as tough as boot leather. I have experienced wonder as I realized that the little boy on the front of my newspaper is holding a picture of his dead father, a picture that I had taken with my camera. I've seen the devastating loss in the eyes of a woman who had lost the love of her life. I've prayed to God to use me to reach out to the women of our squadron, and I have been able to watch as the seeds that He gave me the strength to plant have grown tall and strong.

What I want is for you to see that these women are the backbone of the military. The men are the heroes that risk their lives, but we are the ones who pick up the pieces. I have only a year left to be part of the Marine Corps family and I am determined to spend it working hard, being a little more like Jesus. I want to leave a mark, not for my benefit, but because I am able. These are the shoes that I have chosen to walk in, and I would like others to understand what it is like to work behind the scenes in the lives of our nation's heroes.

AUTHOR BIO

Andrea Cooper has been married to her Marine for three years. He is stationed at Camp Pendleton where he has served for the past four years. Andrea spends much of her time working as part of the Kew Volunteer Network. The Marine Corps organized this system as the main link between the command and the families. During times of war, this network is the only source of accurate information from the squadron to the families left behind. The Iraqi war is no exception.

THROUGH GOD'S EYES

Irene Costilow

"Mrs. Costilow, as an experienced psychologist, my advice is to institutionalize Kelly and Kevin. They are profoundly retarded." His words tore my heart.

I ran out of the psychologist's office, crying uncontrollably. How could he have given me such a report? The words kept resounding in my ears as I drove home. *How could I face this?* Desperate thoughts ran through my mind. *Don't go home. Just run away! Drive into the brick wall and end it all.* This was too much to bear. I loved my twin sons dearly, but I just couldn't deal with this news!

When I pulled into the driveway, I noticed my friend's car. "Irene, I don't know why I'm here. God just told me to come and wait for you." She was an angel sent by God. I collapsed into her arms and cried on her shoulder for hours. She tried to reassure me, "Somehow, God will help you and see you through this." I wasn't sure I believed her, I was pretty angry at God!

I didn't handle Kelly and Kevin's situation very well. I was depressed and lonely, often shaking my fist at God. I was also so angry, grieving the death of a dream for my children's perfect life. For days I would sit in my old, comfy chair and ask God why.

During this time, God spoke to my heart and reminded me how much He loved His Son, Jesus. It hurt Him to see His Son suffer and die. I began to realize that God understood my pain and heartache. God said that He gave His Son, Jesus, to die on the cross for my sins and to give me eternal life. I never really thought this applied to me because I was a good person. However, God gently guided me to see my need for forgiveness. Finally I prayed and asked God to come into my life and to help me with Kelly and Kevin.

After I prayed, I fully expected a miracle, that God would "fix" Kelly and Kevin. I kept watching and waiting for signs of improvement, but nothing changed! Their needs remained the same.

I was in for a big surprise because I noticed that I was the one changing. My attitude became one of patience and acceptance. I began seeing Kelly and Kevin as the most precious gifts that God could have given to me. They are the reason I found Jesus, and for that, I'll forever be thankful. God doesn't make mistakes. He knew what He was doing when He chose to give these special boys to me.

The Bible says: "*Therefore, if anyone is in Christ, he is a new creation; the old is gone, the new has come!*" (II Corinthians 5:17, NIV) That is what happened to me! As a new creation in Christ, I began to see Kelly and Kevin with new eyes, God's eyes.

Kelly and Kevin are 30-years-old now, and live with us in our home. They graduated from special education high school, began driving when they were 19, and they have worked since they were 17. They need our assistance with certain things but for the most part, they are well adjusted, hardworking young men. It thrills me that those little boys, whom the psychologist recommended we institutionalize, get up every day, go to work and pay taxes as honorable American citizens.

They attend church faithfully and are active in their singles class. Last year Kevin bought his first car, a 2002 red Mustang convertible, which he fondly calls his "chick magnet." As you can see, they have truly been a blessing to our lives.

AUTHOR BIO

Irene Costilow resides in Yukon, Oklahoma. She is the Regional Speaker Trainer for Stonecroft Ministries and is a popular speaker for Christian Women's Clubs, retreats, and other women's events.

THE CONCH SHELL

Connie Crider

Mild temperatures filled the air as gentle breezes lifted the coat tails of beach travelers. Orchestrated sounds of breaking waves, screeching sea gulls, joggers' pounding strides, shells crunching under foot, mixed with muffled conversation and laughter provided a sonata for the soul. This mild February day, as drifting sand brushed against my face and salt flavored my lips, was a sign that spring days would soon come. For the brave ones making this pilgrimage to the ocean, it was a reward of tranquility. It was a glorious Carolina day!

Walking along the shoreline, I was struck with a sense of contrast between peace and turmoil in my life. Peace came as a result of being at this place, enjoying God's creation, and taking in the sights, smells and sounds. Turmoil came from an illness that had taken over my life. As I continued walking, tears began to fill my eyes and sadness enveloped my heart and mind. Luckily, I didn't walk alone that day. God was by my side. I whispered a prayer, "God, please help me understand what I've been through and what I'm feeling."

Only a few months had passed since a severe clinical depression had stolen a life of normalcy. As my condition worsened I became a danger to myself and was admitted to a mental health facility. Physically, I had not been allowed to die. Feeling let down by God, I became angry with Him. Having become mentally dead, I also felt spiritually dead. Entering the hospital, I was truly a broken vessel. At that point I was stripped of privacy, freedom, my family, dignity, and the ability to feel safe in a world that had once felt so comfortable. But I have learned that neither environment, time, nor state of mind limits God. Even in that humiliating place, He was at work.

Several days had passed since I completed my twenty-day treatment in the mental health facility. Walking away from the hospital, I was overcome with a need to get away. God had brought me to this beach. He was about to teach me the most valuable lesson of my life.

As I continued to walk, God was touching my heart and mind. From the tears came a feeling of peace, a peace that only He can give. Coming to the end of the beach, I stood in awe at the God I served. While fellowshipping with God, He spoke to me: "Connie, while you may have lost a lot of things during your stay in the hospital, the one thing that couldn't be taken from you was your spirit. I was with you all the time, and I will never leave you."

Gratitude overcame me, and joy filled my soul. The fellowship continued as I headed back to the hotel. Just ahead I saw something sticking out in the surf. As I approached the object, God spoke again, "Connie, pick it up. Let it be My symbol to you that I will always be with you." Once upon the object I could hardly believe my eyes! The object was a whole conch shell about the size of my hand. Even though the shell was whole, it was scarred from being tossed around in the ocean, with a few barnacles attached to it. God was telling me that I was like that shell, whole but scarred, with room for improvement.

Almost one year later, I was drawn back to the same stretch of beach. This time I was a much stronger person, almost recovered, yet still struggling. Again, God accompanied me. After a short while God spoke, "Remember my promise, I'm always with you." Several steps later I looked down and there were two conch shells. One representing God and one representing me, smaller this time but no less significant. Leaning to pick up the shells, I smiled and thanked God for this precious gift. Not only was this a reminder but a gift of encouragement.

The fellowship continued as I walked on. Turning on my headset, I came across a Christian radio station. Stopping to worship, I couldn't help but reflect on how far I had come over the past year. Standing on shore, looking toward the horizon, I was amazed how truly awesome God is. To be His child is a blessing!

A flock of sea gulls glided effortlessly across the surf. Wave after wave rolled to shore as the wind, once again, whipped at my coat tails.

For that one brief moment in time, life was perfect. I stood in God's presence having been reminded of His promise to me. As if on queue, the sun peeked from behind the clouds and *It Is Well* began to play.

"*When peace like a river attendeth my way,. When sorrows like sea billows roll. Whatever my lot, Thou has taught me to say, It is well, it is well with my soul!*"

There have been good and bad times since those walks on the beach. And no matter what the circumstances, God has been right by my side. It's not always easy to find Him, but once found, He gives peace, hope, joy, and love. All I have to do is keep my eyes on Him. I keep my conch shells in a basket in my den. Every time I see them, I smile and inwardly thank God for His promise.

---- AUTHOR BIO ----

Connie Crider lives in Lexington, South Carolina with her husband, Mark and her daughters, Olivia and Amanda. Everyone in the family is an active member at First Baptist of Lexington. Connie enjoys writing, reading, listening to music, watching movies, putting together jigsaw puzzles, crafts, and spending time with family and friends.

Waiting At The Fence

Dean Crowe

"Then you will know the truth, and the truth will set you free."
(John 8:32, NIV)

Late one December afternoon, my husband and I hopped on a plane with several other couples from Atlanta and headed to Nicaragua. Our purpose was to deliver Christmas presents to children at several orphanages. After landing, we went to the mission house and began organizing our gifts for the children. All of us were excited and eager to get to the orphanages the next day.

The next morning we loaded onto a school bus and headed toward our first stop—Moises Orphanage, an all-boy orphanage. Anticipation was high, and we were a bit nervous as we saw the chain link fence that separated Moises from the road. We drove up a wide dirt driveway surrounded by several small, blue-green, cinder block buildings.

Boys of all ages were running around, and their faces broke into big grins when they saw our bus. We were instructed to just start playing with the boys. Our host said after we played for a bit, he would call us together, share the Christmas story and then we would give the gifts. I was excited to be at Moises—after all I have two boys! We poured out of the bus and the games began!

It was then that I heard the Lord whisper, "Wait just a few minutes. There is someone I want you to meet."

I waited, and then I saw him, a shy little boy, about eight-years-old. He hugged a pole, quietly observing all the activity. I went over and said the one word I knew in Spanish, "Hola!"

He smiled, but didn't let go of the pole. I tussled his hair and tickled him. He began to laugh. So I grabbed a ball and tossed it to him. I hadn't met a boy yet who could resist a ball!

We played catch for a few minutes, and then he came over and gently took my hand. He led me over to a concrete wall, motioning for me to sit down. Then he snuggled right up to me. We sat there, smiling at one another. I pointed to myself and told him, "My name is Miss Dean."

He looked up at me with his big brown eyes, smiled and pointed to himself, and said, "Martinez." At that moment, he captured my heart.

We sat there a few minutes, and then he suddenly jumped up and tossed me the ball. We were playing catch again. Then he took my hand again, and we went back to the concrete wall. He motioned for me to sit sown and then he crawled up in my lap again.

My heart started to break. I thought about how much I love to hold each of my boys and that Martinez didn't have a Mama's lap to crawl into when he needed extra love. I held him close. He gazed up at me with those big brown eyes and smiled as he buried his face into my shoulder. I hugged him even tighter, and my heart broke a little more.

Martinez got up and motioned for me to follow him. I did, and he indicated that I should stop and stay where I was standing. I smiled at this boy who was stealing my heart and watched him run full speed ahead through a door in one of the cinder block buildings. After stepping inside for a moment, he came running toward me with something in his hand.

When he got close, I realized it was a very beat up and battered Wiffle bat. But when Martinez showed me the bat, he had such pride in his eyes. I was humbled and broken because I knew that at my house we would have thrown that bat away, yet it was Martinez's most prized possession.

We played ball for a little while, and then it was time to gather together for the Christmas story. Martinez sat in my lap and we smiled at each other as the Christmas story unfolded by pictures. Then it was time for the presents! All the children were as excited as we were. Martinez's name wasn't called until almost the end. There were more children at the orphanage than we thought, so all he received was a shirt and one little matchbox car.

Martinez smiled and examined the car. In the short amount of time I had spent with him, I could tell he was a very bright boy. We went out into the dirt playground of the orphanage, and Martinez drove the car along imaginary dirt roads as I laughed. Then something was said in Spanish, and I knew it was time for us to leave.

Martinez wrapped his hand into mine and walked me toward the bus. Then he stopped and jumped into my arms hugging me and holding onto me with all his might.

Choking back tears, I prayed, "Lord, this is so hard! I love this little guy. He's kind, smart, and sincere. I'd take him home in a second."

Then Martinez took my hand. We continued toward the bus. When we got to the door of the bus, he hopped back up into my arms and looked at me with tears in his eyes. I held him tight and told him that I loved him, that I would always pray for him. I knew he didn't understand English but in my heart, I knew he understood.

As I got on the bus, Martinez's eyes locked with mine as I was going down the aisle to find my seat. Our eyes remained locked and he followed the bus as it drove down the wide dirt driveway to the chain link fence. When he got to the fence, Martinez wrapped his eight-year-old fingers through the fence looking directly at me the entire time. Our eyes remained locked until the bus drove out of sight.

I slumped down in my seat, my heart breaking, and cried out to God, "Why Lord? I want to take him home with me. I love him. This really hurts. Why did you want me to meet Martinez?"

Ever so sweetly and softly, the Lord spoke to my breaking heart: "Dean, I want you to tell others that I am Martinez. I am the One with My fingers wrapped through the chain link fence. I love them, and I am waiting to play with them, to snuggle up close to them, and hold them close. I am waiting to take the beat-up and battered things in their lives and make them a prized possession. I will even take the smallest gift and turn it into a delight. I want them to jump into my arms, and hold I will onto them with all My might because I love them so much. Dean, tell them I am waiting. I am waiting."

──────── AUTHOR BIO ────────

Dean Crowe is a published writer, frequent speaker at
women's events, and Bible study teacher. She has been
married for 20 adventurous years and is the mom of
two wonderful teenage boys. She has written an
in-depth Bible study, Qualities of a Wise Woman.

ONLY BY THE GRACE OF GOD

Melia Dickinson

God's grace has always been a familiar term in my head, but if I were to be honest, very unfamiliar in my heart. Unfamiliar, that is, until two years ago when my brother had convinced me to sign up to go with him overseas with a mission organization that he had been working with for several years. I didn't really want to go on this trip, and I fought the idea for a while, wishing I hadn't made that promise. Eventually, though, the Lord won the battle, and the excuses and fears were quickly replaced with an excitement as the summer drew near. I wasn't really sure what to expect. I knew we were going into closed countries where missionaries were not allowed, and therefore, were going to do a different type of evangelism than the normal street performances. I didn't, however, expect that I would learn such an unforgettable lesson in God's grace that is still difficult for me to talk about today.

I signed up for the "Blitz Asia" team, which went to two different countries in East Asia. Living in the US, I've always known I was blessed, but as we arrived and began our ministry, I began to really see just how fortunate I am. Looking around and seeing the poverty was heartbreaking. There was trash and human waste everywhere. Beggars and street children were rampant. I found myself constantly thanking God that this was not my life.

Perhaps the hardest slap in the face that summer was the day we spent at an orphanage. I was adopted from Korea as an infant, so orphaned children have always held a special place in my heart. I was thrilled to be able to go in and show these kids love, even if it was only for a few hours. I don't think that I was prepared, however, for the emotion of it all. I walked into the room I was assigned to and nearly lost control. I hadn't expected to grow so attached to each child at the first glimpse.

I found myself drawn to a crib where a baby lay crying. I picked her up and held her close. While many of the children in this room were physically and/or mentally handicapped, I could see nothing wrong with this baby...except that she was a girl. My heart swelled and I asked God for a miracle—that somehow she would be spared from feeling the pain of being unloved either through adoption or the dulling of her senses. The other child I was drawn to was another baby girl who was so severely malnourished that she had to be fed intravenously through her head since her arms and legs were so shrunken. I asked the nurse if I could hold her. I got a response I recognized, so I sat on the floor next to her and held her hand and stroked her as she cried. Finally, the nurse walked over to the crib, roughly wrapped her and picked her up, handing her to me. I carried her gently to a corner, half terrified I'd break this fragile little life. For over an hour I cradled her and prayed for her, pleading with the Lord to show mercy on her. Each time she cried, I began to sing to her and she would stop, her blank gray eyes searching for mine. As the time came to go, I reluctantly set her back in her bed and said a blessing over each child in the room. I left quickly so as not to share my tears with the children.

As we returned to the place we were staying, I found myself not thanking God for my life, but asking Him why He had chosen to rescue me from that life. I could not comprehend the fact that He would choose me. Out of all the orphaned children, why had He chosen me?

Throughout our emotional team debriefing of the day, I remained deep in thought, still unable to speak. The comment was made that we should thank God because in all actuality, any one of those children could have been one of us. Later, as I reflected on that, it hit me. Yes, any one of those children could very well have been me; statistically, it should have been me. But, the reality of it is this: it's not me. I'm not living that life. God did choose me, and He chose me because He knew of a task that only I could fulfill. Ashamed of my impudence in questioning Him, I fell before Him asking forgiveness. Then I thanked Him over and over again for choosing me.

I returned home that summer a changed person. When I think back to how close I was to not going on that trip, I almost shudder because I hate to think of what my life would be like today. I am forever grateful that God saw fit for me to be on that trip if for no other reason than to learn an emotional lesson on grace through two beautiful baby girls, whose faces are still clearly etched in my mind. My very thought process has changed. I live my life differently knowing that everything I have, every luxury, big or small, is only by the grace of God. My very existence as I know it – it's only by the grace of God. Do I deserve it? Absolutely not. But that's the beauty of grace.

─── AUTHOR BIO ───

Melia Dickinson, 21, resides in Westminster, Colorado where she is currently teaching elementary computers and secondary drama at a Christian school.

God's Provision in a Time of Unemployment

Beth Doucette

I sit waiting for the phone to ring. Will my agencies come up with a job for me? Will one of the employers I've interviewed with make me an offer? Will the labor department be able to help me out?

I try to relax and not think about my bills. I need groceries. The car needs an oil change. The cat needs food. Will I have the money for the car note, the insurance, the rent?

Lord, this is Your problem. You've told me to cast all my cares on You. Okay, here they come! I wonder why it's so hard to trust a God who has provided for me before so many times. Perhaps I need to remind myself.

My income tax check covered the last of my medical bills for last year. My friend's unexpected gift of $60 in December covered my electric bill for that month. The same friend cheerfully gave me groceries from her own cabinets. Another friend did the same and offered to help me with my car note for last month. There is the co-choir member who gave me $20 because she wanted to bless me. There is the truck driving couple who pays me to feed their fish and gave me cat food and eggs. There is my family, who sent me an unexpected gift of $50, which paid for groceries that week. They also paid for my plane trips home for the holidays, out of their own need.

And then there is the computer. I told God that if He wanted me to have one, He would have to provide it. Why was it so surprising when He did just that through another friend whose boss was giving it away?

I suppose the $50 balance in my checking account and the lack of permanent employment shouldn't scare me. He is a God who is able and who does care and provides. I just wish the process of learning to trust was already over. I suppose though, that I wouldn't know if I trusted Him if challenges didn't come up.

Lord, please help me to be trusting and grateful as I wait on Your provision in a time of unemployment.

──────── AUTHOR BIO ────────

Beth Doucette is a freelance writer, originally from New England, who has lived in Nashville, Tennessee since 1991. She attends Christ Church where she is a member of the choir, a communion steward, and works with her drama group. She shares her apartment with her cat, Mocha.

SHADOWS

Janet Dowty

It was long ago, and the night was dark and stormy. The wind howled around the old stone house, but we felt safe within its thick walls.

My brother, sister, and I sat on the window seat with the heavy curtains closed behind us, watching the storm. It was fascinating to see debris blow up to the window two stories high, the rain falling sideways, and a brave individual attempting to walk, reaching for street lights, walls, and a garden gate as he struggled home.

The windowpane was ice cold, and it didn't take us long to discover that if we blew on it, we could use our buttons to draw a pattern then watch it freeze just like Jack Frost. It was there that our mother discovered us, surprised to find us playing unafraid on such a winter's night.

Our discontent at being told it was bedtime quickly changed to glee as we were informed Daddy had built a fire in our room due to the bitter weather. We scurried into bed and hugged our hot water bottles, delighting in the bright cozy room. Light from the fire danced all over the ceiling and we soon made a game of it, imagining light-bright, happy fairies, dancing and playing in a spring garden. It was so much fun, and we felt as warm as toast.

Suddenly a log slid down on the coals, and the room turned dark. The dancing fairies became dark evil demons reaching out to try and grab us. Our childish fun quickly turned to fear and dread of the dark shadows and the howling wind.

We called for our mother, and she came, telling us little that children ought to be asleep by now. We responded in a chorus "but we are scared of the dark shadows!"

"Why you silly sausages," said our mother. "Have you forgotten Jesus is in the shadows? He is here right now." She squatted down and, stirring the fire, she sang to us. We had heard it many times before:

Standing somewhere in the shadows you'll find Jesus.
He's the only one who cares and understands.
Standing somewhere in the shadows you will find Him.
And you'll know Him by the nail prints in His hands.

Can you wonder?
Can you wonder?
Can you wonder why it is I love Him so?
When I think of all He's done
For me, the guilty one.
Can you wonder why it is I love Him so!

I felt so ashamed. "Stupid! Stupid! Stupid!" I said to myself.
My mother soon left the room, and I lay awake for a long time
listening to the quiet breathing sounds of my sleeping brother and sister.

Then I prayed, "No matter how old I am, or where I may be,
I will never again be afraid in the dark and the shadows because
I know You are there."

More than twenty years, and many miles later, I lay on the floor.
The windows were boarded and the bedroom doors all closed. I could
hear the quiet breathing sounds of my sleeping children huddled close
together on the hallway floor. I was tired. I had washed all the clothes
in the house, cooked all the perishable food, and filled every available
container with water. The power was out now, and a hurricane blew
around us. My husband was listening to his ham radio as the kerosene
lamp cast its shadows on the ceiling. I watched those shadows and
was filled with peace. Then I remembered. I remembered those little
children on that stormy night. The fire and the shadows and, my
mother's song.

I watched the shadows. I heard the howling hurricane. And I fell
asleep because I knew He was there.

──────── AUTHOR BIO ────────
Janet Dowty lives in Ladson, South Carolina. She is
a housewife, mother of nine, and granny to one.

JESUS WEPT IN MY PLACE

Christine Dunaway

At the age of twenty-two, there is not a single one of the ten commandments that I have not broken. I have lied, stolen, lived a promiscuous life, and the list goes on. I am certainly not proud of my past, yet because of my faith in Jesus Christ I have hope for both tomorrow and for eternity. It is only because of God's great mercy that I am alive to tell this story today. If by doing so, I can reach one unbeliever, my life's mission will have been accomplished.

I was born in 1980 to a young couple on a military base in Athens, Greece. My mother was the daughter of Mexican immigrants to America and my father was an aspiring Air Force recruit. Both were converts to Christianity, yet each carried vast amounts of emotional baggage from their childhood. At a very early age, I remember placing my faith in Christ. However, as time went on and my parents' marriage drifted onto the rocks, I began to question God's place in our lives. While they had always tried to raise me appropriately, I had also learned about rejection and holding onto bitterness. I became self-sufficient, not turning to God in times of pain and need. Slowly, but surely, the enemy built walls up around my heart. These walls buffered me from the pain of insecurity.

When I was fifteen-years-old, my parents went through a bitter divorce. The courts placed me with my father, and we moved from Virginia to Texas. My whole life was turned upside down at the most vulnerable time. My father had always been loving and devoted to me, but now he became consumed by work, women, and his own pain. Though I never really doubted his love for me, I did wonder what he thought about where my life was headed. I truly believe that he did see my turmoil, but perhaps did not know what to say or how to say it.

Just after my sixteenth birthday, I lost my virginity and began drinking heavily. Getting high and sneaking out at night became a way of life. Just as my life began to spiral out of control, I met Joe.

He was the silent, mysterious type. His hard exterior masked a hurting heart. Naturally, we were attracted to each other instantly. *Perhaps we can help each other*, I reasoned. Three months later I became pregnant. I never tried not to. I suppose I believed that a child, my child, would always love me unconditionally.

Joe and I moved into an apartment together, and he got a job. I delivered a healthy baby boy on December 15th, 1998, and we named him after the angel Gabriel. Sadly, Joe and I did not remain a happy couple. He couldn't keep a steady job and I was often forced to steal formula and diapers for my son. He paraded his other girlfriends shamelessly in front of me, calling me names and making me feel worthless. I begged him with my whole heart to love me. I stayed with him because I thought it was what was best for my son.

Despite all these challenges, I managed to graduate from high school in 1999. Joe was rarely home, and when he was, he was stoned. Gabriel was just six months old when my whole world came crashing down.

The at-home pregnancy test was once again positive. Joe was completely overwhelmed and left me for another woman. I then had a very hard choice to make. I had no one I could turn to. My father had once told me that he would disown me if I ever had another child out of wedlock. My mother and I had a volatile relationship at best. God was a million miles away. All my friends had written me off as a lost cause.

I made the most painful decision of my life without telling anyone. I had an abortion at seven weeks. My unborn child's heart was already beating, and mine was completely broken. I knew in my spirit that abortion was murder, but my head told me to think of Gabriel. I could not afford to feed and clothe him, much less a second child.

Joe felt guilty for what had happened and came crawling back home. He promised he would change. I took him back because I felt like I deserved no better. Two eventful years passed, full of pain and broken promises.

On Easter Sunday, 2001 the unthinkable happened. I was pregnant for the third time. This time, I swore I would do right by my child. When I informed Joe of the new development, he demanded that I have another abortion. I adamantly refused, and he beat me. He left me bruised physically, but stronger emotionally. I threw him out of my home and began to earnestly seek God's face for the first time in years. I knew I had made a mess out of my life and I knew I had to change.

It was during this important transitional period that God brought back into my life an old friend from my past. Ultimately this best friend would become my husband. I had first met Tim around the time my parents split up. He was a good old southern boy, a Christian, and the one person who had never quite given up on me. When I told him what was happening, he encouraged me to make a prayerful decision. God gave me an inner strength that I had never known before, and I began to research open adoption.

That is when I found Buckner Maternity and Adoption in Dallas, Texas. They took me under their wings, counseled both little Gabriel and myself, and explained how open adoption could work. They told me I could choose a Christian family, meet them, and even share my heart with them. This was the answer to my prayers. I perused countless profiles for prospective families and chose one. The family was perfect, and we bonded instantly! As the birth of my second son drew near, Tim became my rock. Even though he was overseas serving in the Navy, he was still there for me. There is no telling how many phone cards we used, and during those trying months, I began to love him.

On December 6th, 2001, Daniel made his triumphant entrance into our lives. I remember looking into his eyes and tears of joy streaming down my face. I loved him so much, yet I knew he was a gift from God that was meant to be shared. I have never felt such peace as when I placed him into his new family's waiting arms. Some people have told me that I didn't love my son enough to keep him. But I say I loved my son enough to think of his needs over mine. I loved him enough to carefully select two wonderful parents as my gift to him. I loved him enough to entrust him into their care. Every time I see Daniel now, I heal a little bit more. Each time I am able to confront the emptiness, it fills up with joy in my decision.

Tim and I were recently married and are now stationed in Hawaii. We strive daily to teach Gabriel of God's love and grace. Daniel is now about to turn two, and will never wonder who I am, or why I did what I did. Better still, he has a big brother who adores him. We are like an extended family, and we are never more than a phone call away. Though my story has not always been a happy one, I pray that it will touch lives. No one truly understands God's sacrificial love like a birth mother. We really are all adopted children, for while we were yet sinners, Christ died for us. God has brought me from the lowest point and given me eagle's wings. He can do that for anyone. I could sit here and dwell on the horrible pain of my experiences, but the awesome truth is that Jesus wept in my place.

─── AUTHOR BIO ───

Christine Dunaway lives in Hawaii with her husband and son. She is a volunteer counselor at a crisis pregnancy center and enjoys writing and going to the beach.

THE GOD OF MIRACLES

Darlene Eastes

The overhead light from the incubator cast an angelic glow
over baby John's tiny body. It was quiet and dark in the pediatric unit
despite the many premature babies that had been born. I stood, gazing
at the miracle before me. My nephew, who had been so anxiously
awaited, was born at twenty-six weeks.

My mind jogged back to when my sister first told us she was
pregnant. We were all excited since this was going to be the first
grandchild born into our family of five girls. I envisioned a bright
and chubby baby to spoil whenever I wanted. Instead, I had traveled
for hours to be with my sister after her emergency c-section and was
standing before my nephew who barely weighed over a pound.

The music box chimed out *Jesus Loves Me* while I bit my lip to
fight back tears. I cried out to God, "Why? I don't understand. It's not
supposed to be this way." He looked so tiny and helpless. I was almost
afraid to breathe. Through my tears, I heard God's voice resounding
in my ears, "Do you trust me?" This was not the first time I had heard
him ask. There had been issues with money, relationships, and
decisions in which I needed to relinquish control, but never had
I trusted him to pull a life from the jaws of death.

The music box chime ended, and drowning the silence now was
the rapid beeping of the apnea monitor just above my head. Politely
a nurse came by and gave John a gentle shaking.

"What is that?" I asked. She responded, "Most premature babies
have apnea. They sleep and forget to breathe. We just give them
a little nudge to remind them." My outlook on the situation grew
even grimmer. Again, God's voice came, "Do you trust me?" I thought
of everything that He had done for me. The nights that I had no one,
but He was there; the times He cared for me and loved me
unconditionally. "Yes." I answered. "I will trust You."

Peace and a new boldness of faith came upon me. Physically, there was nothing I could do for John, but I could pray for him. I could believe God. So, from that moment on, the decision was made. I was going to believe God no matter what the situation looked like. Some people called it denial. There was no denying that the outward circumstances looked impossible, but I chose to trust God and have faith that he was bigger than any problem that John would face. The Bible became my best friend. I recalled the saints of old who faced impossible circumstances: Abraham, Noah, Moses, Joseph, Daniel, Esther, Paul and even Jesus himself. Their faith and perseverance became comfort and inspiration to me.

At the time, my sister and I were staying at a nearby Ronald McDonald House. We quickly became connected with each family staying there. Though each situation was different, the effects were similar. There were tired bodies, broken spirits and hearts full of anxiety. Yet at night when I would lie in the bed so unfamiliar to me and lift my prayers of faith, the presence of God would surround me and hope would enter my heart.

Each day we would walk the short distance to the hospital, and every day they would tell us that John had gained an ounce overnight. In our excitement they would remind us that most babies who were as premature as John were prone to infection, and to become joyful was to only bring ourselves to a place of great disappointment. I would only smile knowing that God was in control and he was just proving it to me.

Every day from then on was touch and go. Some days he would gain weight; some days he would lose weight. On one occasion he had lost weight overnight and had several apnea occurrences. I could tell that it was weighing heavy on my sister's heart. The nurse on duty walked up to the incubator admiring the *Jesus Loves Me* musical toy block the aunts had purchased for him.

She smiled. "That's wonderful."

I nodded.

"John, what a strong, solid name, it fits him perfectly," the nurse said. The gold cross around her neck seemed to illuminate when she smiled and winked. I almost gasped at the love of Christ I saw on her face.

Learning to trust God with a life as fragile as a baby born at twenty-six weeks was one of the hardest trials I've ever faced. Seems silly when I think about it. The God who cut a dry path through a raging sea, the God who made the sun stand still, the God who took a lowly shepherd boy, five stones and a sling shot and made him a warrior, the God who fed over five thousand with two fish and five loaves of bread, is the same God who cupped his massive hands gently around a frail body and breathed life. The same God who laid his hands upon the lepers, the outcasts, the lame, placed his hands upon my heart and said "Fear not, only believe."

Today, John is a healthy, talkative, and intelligent seven-year-old. Every time I look at him I remember the past. He was the best teacher I've ever had. He taught me about faith, he taught me that God cares, he taught me that we are not here by mistake or chance, but by the grace and love of God. Most importantly, he taught me humility. For apart from God, I can do nothing, but with him nothing will be impossible. I am not in control, but when I loosen the grip from those things I cling to so tightly, His tender voice will cut through the icy sting of disappointment and give me the courage, strength, and faith to face the trials of life head on.

One day someone asked me if I believed in miracles. I thought for a moment. "No." I answered to the surprise of the one who asked. I continued, "I believe in the God of miracles."

— Author Bio —

Darlene Eastes lives in Indianapolis, Indiana. She enjoys writing, watching movies, and spending time with friends and family.

A CRUMB FROM THE MASTER'S TABLE

Allison Garner

I was jolted awake in the middle of the night by a sound most
mothers dread, but instantly recognize. My eldest daughter, Heather,
was sick and had wandered to my bedside. Pushing the wastebasket in
her direction, I waited for the retching that never came.

What I didn't know at the time was that she had experienced her
first mild seizure. I dismissed the incident as a fluke thing and went
about life as usual.

Eighteen months later, another similar episode prompted me into
action. I brought Heather to her doctor and she had an EEG, then an
MRI. The results showed a seizure disorder that could be easily treated
with medication. Once again, I went about my life as before.

It soon became apparent, though, that things had changed
dramatically. Up until this time, Heather had been a good student, but
was now receiving Cs and Ds. She would forget to write down assign-
ments, do them, and turn them in the next day. No amount of
pleading, encouraging or threatening on my part changed her
performance at school. I felt helpless, alone, and turned to God as a
source of comfort and strength. Truthfully, I didn't immediately feel
His presence, but not because He hadn't moved.

Over the previous seventeen years, intimacy between God and me
had diminished. No longer seeking His presence on a daily basis, I
would come to Him only as I did now, in trouble and needing assistance. My emotional state was not helped by the fact I was a perform-
ance-motivated individual, feeling acceptance and approval from God
and others on the basis of what I did, not for whom I was. A new
sense of powerlessness came over me. I had wandered so far away
from the Lord. My thoughts were filled with questions like, *Why would
Jesus help me? What had I done lately for Him?*

Those questions haunted me as I attempted various solutions on
my own, eventually realizing the medication not only prevented my

daughter's seizures, but also caused forgetfulness and cloudy thinking. Withdrawing the drug meant risking another episode, and poor performance at school appeared the likely result if she continued her dosage. There was only one other solution in my mind, yet it seemed too big to hope for or even imagine. God *could* heal Heather. But *would* He?

I asked my friends from Bible Study to join me in prayer for Heather's healing. Then I called her neurologist to see if she would be willing to do another EEG. Encouraged that she agreed, I scheduled a date. I next approached my pastor and requested healing prayer for Heather. But all the while in the back of my mind, the question remained, *Will God do this for me?*

I felt much like the Canaanite woman who came to Jesus on behalf of her demon-possessed daughter. This mother, like myself, knew she was not worthy to ask Him for healing, but in her desperation, came anyway. She even anticipated Jesus' response: *"He replied, 'It is not right to take the children's bread and toss it to their dogs.'"*

"Yes, Lord," she said, "but even the dogs eat the crumbs that fall from their masters' table." (Matthew 15:26 & 27, NIV) She had faith that Jesus would honor her request in spite of her unworthiness. Did I?

The healing ministry of my church is based on what is written in James 5:14 (NIV). *"Is any one of you sick? He should call the elders of the church to pray over him and anoint him with oil in the name of the Lord."* The anointing and prayer time with my daughter, pastor and elders of the church was special for all of us. Some of the elders had known Heather from birth, and their prayers reflected their father-like concern. I truly felt the Lord's presence in my pastor's office that Sunday morning. Regardless of how God answered our request for healing, I knew my relationship with Him had to change.

The following Tuesday morning, Heather and I arrived promptly for the EEG appointment. Results of the test, I was told, would be available after a week, and nine days later, a brief recorded phone message came from the neurologist. The EEG was normal; please call if there were any questions. That same day, I began the process of weaning Heather from her medication.

It took a while for the full impact of what God had done to sink into my heart. Of course, I always knew Jesus, the Great Physician, could heal my daughter. That had never been an issue with me. What tripped me up was thinking that somehow I had to earn this favor from Him.

God, in His mercy, met me where I was and poured out an undeserved blessing. Jesus performed this miracle, not because it was merited, but in demonstration of His abundant love and grace for me. This fact did not escape my attention.

I wish I could say my daughter returned to her former self. While it is true that she never had another seizure, the year of medication has taken its toll. Her grades have never been what they once were.

On the other hand, I did not return to my former self either. A renewed "first love" was born out of that experience, and my intimacy with the Lord grows deeper each day. Five years have passed, yet my eyes still fill with tears whenever I share my story. How could someone not be similarly impacted? It is my earnest prayer that I never forget this crumb that fell from the Master's table.

AUTHOR BIO

Allison Garner (Stine) has been married to Alan for 21 years, and they live in Simi Valley, California with their teenage daughters, Heather and Katheryn. Allison is currently a Children's Director for Community Bible Study and enjoys needlework and home canning. She has won several blue ribbons at the County Fair, most notably for her Pomegranate Jelly.

AN UNEXPECTED GIFT WRAPPED
IN GOD'S GRACE

Kelly Gerken

Sometimes what I think I need isn't even close to what God has in store for me. My family and I were given the most valuable gift which came in a package we never would have chosen or expected.

Our story begins with my second pregnancy. At our first doctor's appointment an ultrasound confirmed that I was carrying twins! We were overwhelmed with joy and fear!

By the twenty-second week of pregnancy, I was admitted to the hospital to stop labor pains. After several days of battling the labor with magnesium sulfate, an ultrasound confirmed a problem with the pregnancy, and I was sent to a high-risk specialist at another hospital. The specialist determined that our twin daughters had a condition known as twin-to-twin transfusion syndrome, where one baby gets too much nourishment and the other baby does not get enough. They performed amniocentesis procedures to remove the excess fluid from the sac that carried the babies. I remained in the hospital for several more days. During the many ultrasounds performed, we would watch as Faith sucked her thumb and Grace swam wildly about. We chose the names Faith and Grace from Ephesians 3:8. How we prayed that they would be saved.

At twenty-six weeks, an ultrasound showed that the hearts of Faith and Grace, who had struggled so to survive, were no longer beating. The pain and shock of that loss, the word stillborn, the labor and the funeral plans were all a blur, as if happening to someone else.

During my labor I looked out the window and watched snowflakes falling silently, so perfect and beautiful, just like I imagined our daughters would be. When they were born, we held them and wept, and I sang *Amazing Grace*. Although they were bruised and broken, all I could see was their indescribable beauty. I had prayed that God would save them and I realized that He had saved them, just not the way I had in mind. They were in heaven, perfect and without suffering, complete and safe.

The grief that followed was a relentless roller coaster. My physical and emotional health were in desperate need of healing. I questioned the strength of my faith. I didn't yet realize that God's strength is made perfect in our weakness.

A year later, we conceived our fourth child. We were filled with apprehension and hope. An ultrasound in mid-pregnancy indicated an inadequate amount of amniotic fluid. I was sent to a specialist who confirmed through a variety of tests that our baby probably had a fatal condition known as Potter's Syndrome, where babies have a lack of amniotic fluid due to the absence of kidneys. The inadequate amounts of amniotic fluid leave the baby's lungs unable to properly develop, and they cannot function. There is no chance of survival.

We felt forsaken. The darkness of that rainy day was consuming and hideous. Why was this happening to us again?

The next topic that the doctor presents to a couple in this situation is "The choice"—whether or not to terminate the pregnancy. From a medical perspective, this seemed like the obvious choice. There was no chance of the baby's survival and the more he grew, the more likely he would be harmed physically due to the limited space caused by lack of fluid.

It was Holy Week, when we had to choose the fate of our unborn child, a son, as if we were qualified to do such a thing. I was afraid for the pain our family would face again, and afraid for the possible harm caused to the baby if he were to remain in my womb. I cried out to the Lord night and day, praying, weeping, searching the Scriptures for the answer. And He answered me.

As I read the Easter story, I came to the part where Pontius Pilate washes his hands of Jesus' situation because he does not want the blood on his hands. I realized that if we made this choice, we would have the blood of our child on our hands. There would be no quick escape from the pain and suffering. Instead it would have been a pain that may never heal because we would have to live with the guilt of it having been our choice. But, if we left the situation in God's hands, He would make a path for us to healing and restoration. Maybe He would even choose to save our son. So we put the situation in His capable hands, trusting Him to care for all of us.

The next four months tested our faith constantly. We prayed fervently for a miracle, hoping and wishing, fearing that staying could be causing physical harm and deformities to our baby. It was a great strain on our family. I spent time planning his funeral and yet, still somehow hoping that God would give us a miracle and save him.

We chose the name Thomas for our son because through this journey, we learned about believing God without seeing. We learned that being faithful doesn't mean not feeling doubt or fear. Faith is believing God's promises, clinging to His truth anyway, when you're most afraid and filled with doubt and questions. Still believing when the answer is not what you want to hear or when there seems to be no answer at all.

When the moment came for me to deliver Thomas, it was clear that God's grace truly was sufficient for us. While a team of experts worked to save Thomas, I prayed and cried out to the Lord. I was immediately filled with that peace that surpasses all human understanding. The Lord was with us, so close that I could feel His presence, as if I could reach out and touch Him.

Although God did not work the kind of miracle that I had asked for, there were miracles that day. Thomas was beautiful! He was with us for six hours. We were able to hold him and pray over him. There were no scars on him and his limbs were intact. There was no evidence that remaining pregnant without amniotic fluid had harmed him in any way!

During the last moments of Thomas' life, I rocked him and began singing to him and worshipping. As he left this earth, it occurred to me that I had been given a great privilege. I had been chosen to sing to this beautiful baby as he went straight from my arms to the arms of Jesus. I was bathed in peace and an indescribable joy. It was worth a lifetime of being Thomas' mother to be the one who held him and sang to him on his way to heaven. I have never felt closer to Jesus than in that moment. I knew that He existed in a way that I never had known before. His promises are real, and He will not leave us or forsake us.

I could never have envisioned in my limited human mind that He would have such an experience waiting for me at the end of this journey.

I was truly blessed among women that day, blessed among Mothers.

Isaiah 49:16 says *"...I will not forget you! See, I have engraved you on the palms of my hands; your walls are ever before me."*

Author Bio

Kelly Gerken lives in Deshler, Ohio with her husband Tim and their two children, Timothy and James. She teaches Sunday school, co-leads a Moms In Touch group, and is co-founder of the Women's Edge Newsletter. She enjoys spending time with family, singing in church, studying God's Word, and writing.

STEPPING INTO THE LIGHT

Mandy Harris

I was raised in a Christian home, but we stopped going to church when I was in third grade. I became depressed in the middle of sixth grade, and although I wasn't really a Christian and neither was my family then, I still believed in God. But I thought He had abandoned me. I was all alone and depressed. I didn't want to get out of bed in the morning. I hated myself so much.

I started cutting myself in seventh grade. I did it to take away the emotional pain, and I felt like I deserved the pain because I hated myself. All I thought about was cutting. I thought that God, if He existed, had forgotten about me for sure. I felt like I was falling into a deep, never-ending hole of depression. It consumed my thoughts. I just wanted to die. I was so suicidal that I almost took my life.

That summer after seventh grade, I went to Camp Muscatine. It was a day-camp that a local church had put on for teenagers for three days. I felt God there, and everyone was so loving. God touched me so much there. I had never felt anything like that before in my life. The people there had something I was missing, and I wanted very badly what they had. I realized that God loved me and wanted to be there for me, and I rededicated my life to Christ at the camp.

God gave me the courage to reach out and get help for my depression and self-injury soon after that. But when my parents found out about my depression and cutting in eighth grade, it became much worse. I hated life. I thought things would get better instantly, but I was wrong. Being home was horrible because they were in denial. The medication didn't take all the depression away, and I still wanted to cut myself. I was addicted to cutting and never really stopped. I felt alone.

A friend invited me to a church (the same church that had put on the camp that summer) and the people welcomed me and were so friendly. I felt something different I'd never felt before. It was so awesome. Ever since camp, I had been praying that God would help me out of the depression and bring me to a church. I longed for the love and the sense of the presence of God that I had felt that summer at Camp Muscatine. I remember listening to the song *Better is One Day in Your Courts* and hoping that one day I would be able to be in a church with other believers, and finally I was there.

About two months after I started going to the church every Wednesday, I told the youth pastor about my depression. He talked to my parents and told them about a Christian therapist they knew (she's helped me so much). And a week later, my parents started going to the church too. God has filled me with something I never knew I could have. I still struggle with depression and cutting, but He gives me something to hang on to. I know I'm never alone because He's always there, even when I don't feel like He's there. I realized that I needed to tell someone about my depression, and that even though it got worse, God was there and helped me through it. And I'm so glad I got help.

I changed so much after I gave my life to God. I finally knew I wasn't alone. I used to listen to any music that had lyrics about depression, suicide, and cutting. Now I listen to Christian music that encourages me and praises God.

My family and I started to spend a lot of time at church. My family has even gotten much closer, and they are very supportive of me. Even the people I admired has changed. I used to want to be like the popular girls at school. I would have given anything to be popular, and I wanted to be just like them. But I started to look up to other Christian teens in the youth group, and I admired how willing they were to live their life for Christ. I wanted to be more like them and more like Christ.

God has done so much in my life, and He continues to work on me and help me. I still struggle with depression. I've stopped cutting like I use to, but I still struggle with it. God is always there, and gives me hope even in my darkest times, and I know even though sometimes He feels a thousand miles away, He's still there holding me.

Author Bio
Mandy Harris is 15-years-old. She lives in Muscatine,
Iowa with her mom, dad, and younger sister, Mindy.
She is involved in her youth group, church activities,
and color guard. She enjoys writing poetry and stories,
listening to Christian music, and being with her friends.

ANGEL AT THE BUS

Derek Hastings

January 5, 1980 dawned cold and cloudy; snow gently fell on the empty street. Only a few days earlier I had publicly acknowledged Jesus Christ as my Lord and Savior. And that day, I was to catch a city bus that would take me to the Port Authority in New York City and on to Coast Guard training in Yorktown. Nancy and I moved slowly down that morning, trying not to think of the four months we would be apart.

Finally, with my duffel bag, a carry-on and my new Bible in the car, we headed for the bus station. About five minutes before the bus was scheduled to arrive, I realized I had left my uniform hat back at the house. Nancy jumped in the car and drove back to get it, leaving me to wait for the bus. By the time she returned, I had missed the bus that would have allowed me to make connections in New York.

I finally boarded the next bus and arrived at the Port Authority precisely at 10:30 am, exactly the time the connecting bus was to leave. I jumped off in a panic, my mind swimming with images of showing up late for Officer Candidate School.

Once inside, I found the ticket area, got in line and bought my ticket. My bus, they said, was leaving from Gate 36. I ran the full length of the building before I saw a sign that indicated that Gate 36 was downstairs and all the way back at the other end.

I glanced down at my watch. It was 10:45 am! I was fifteen minutes late, and there were no other people waiting to board! I crashed into the metal door with all the weight of my body and luggage. There sat the bus, engine idling.

"Is this the bus to Baltimore?" I asked breathlessly as the driver opened the door.

"Yes, it is," he replied.

The man climbed down from his seat and proceeded to the cargo compartment to stow my bag. He was a big man, over six feet tall with broad shoulders, a big smile and white hair. As I turned to climb into the bus, he asked, "What's that book you have there?"

"It's my new Bible," I replied. "I just bought it last weekend."

The driver smiled. "Read Psalm 91:11 and you will see why I waited for you."

"What?" I exclaimed, exhausted from the excitement.

"Read Psalm 91:11 and you will see why I waited for you," he repeated.

I climbed on board, found a seat on the left side about halfway back near the window and opened my Bible. *"For he will command his angels concerning you to guard you in all your ways."*

I looked up. The driver was watching me in the large rearview mirror.

"Beautiful, isn't it?" he said as our eyes met.

Sometime later, in Baltimore, I watched as the bus pulled out of the station and stopped at a traffic signal a short distance down the road. The driver turned, locked eyes with me and, with another big smile, waved. Amazed, I waved back.

When I finally reached the motel, I called Nancy and told her about the incident on the bus.

"Maybe the man was your guardian angel," she suggested.

At first such a thing was difficult to believe, but when I thought about it, I realized that I had not pre-purchased my tickets and no one knew I was coming. Although I arrived almost fifteen minutes past the departure time, the driver said he had specifically waited just for me! And, what's more, he had waited because God had commanded His angels to guard me along my way.

Throughout the years I have held on to this memory as a very personal and special gift from my Heavenly Father. I believe the Lord sent His angel to establish in my heart whose child I had become.

Author Bio

Derek Hastings is a Certified Financial Planner in Chico, California. He is married to a wonderful wife Nancy, and has three children, Trevor, Justin, and Lauren.

An Appointment in the Air

Susanne Horn

In the middle of the Pacific Ocean, on the island where my husband worked for an airline, God started a transformation in my life. I had a fear of flying. In fact, it went beyond fear into the realm of panic attacks at the thought of flying. My husband, my daughter, and I were moving back to the States after spending over four years on Guam.

I had gotten some relaxants from the doctor to aid me in my flight. The bottle said to take one half to one tablet every eight hours as needed. My husband was at work and would come home later to take me to the airport. He had decided to fly with my daughter later because he thought I wouldn't be as afraid to fly if I did not have my daughter with me. I could just concentrate on myself.

All of a sudden, terrible thoughts came into my head. Darkness invaded the apartment and enveloped me, bringing me to my knees. I could do nothing but curl up on the floor in a fetal position and sob aloud. The only word I could say was "Jesus!" over and over again. I had a complete and total breakdown. Fear surrounded me. I wanted so much to stop this feeling that I dragged myself up to the counter where the medication was. I started to swallow tablets just to try to escape the darkness. I had taken four tablets and had more in my hand when my husband walked in the door, home early from work. God sent him to help me when I most needed it.

I did not overdose, but I became very sleepy and slept almost the whole eight-hour flight from Honolulu. God provided a woman from our church who just happened to be on that flight. She helped guide me to a special room at the Honolulu airport to sleep until my husband and daughter joined me there to pick me up. Then I flew from Honolulu to California with my family.

After we moved to Texas, three other women in my apartment complex formed a small prayer group with me, and God showed me it was time to overcome my fear of flying. My family planned a trip to Minnesota, and the ladies in the prayer group decided to write me short notes of encouragement with songs to sing and scripture verses to read on the flight. They gave me six for the way up and six for the way back. Renee told me, "I can't wait to see what God is going to do!"

The flight up was wonderful. We had a good visit with family in Minnesota, and were scheduled to fly back down to Houston on Sunday at noon. Saturday, my daughter got sick and threw up all night. I got virtually no sleep. She was fine in the morning, but now I was sick. I was tempted to take a later flight home, partly because I was sick and partly because the fear was gripping me again. But I just wanted to get home, so the three of us headed for the airport and boarded the plane.

The plane was crowded, so my husband and I were separated, and I sat in the middle seat with a lady to my left. We started to talk, and she was very friendly. She was from England and here in the States on business. She would fly to Houston and then home to England. Her name was Cathy. I told her of my fear of flying, the notes with Bible verses and that Jesus was my Lord and Savior. I wished I had a gospel tract to share Jesus with her. Cathy said she was not a religious person and that she only went to the Church of England once or twice a year.

I had only read three of Renee's six letters to me. As the flight descended, the Holy Spirit prompted me to give Cathy one of Renee's unopened letters. I knew it was the letter that had a cross drawn on the front and said "Because He first loved us...."

I gave her the sealed envelope and said, "Here is one of the letters my friend wrote me. I don't know what's in it, but whatever it is, it will bless you." She accepted and said she would read it. I said, "Goodbye and God go with you." She smiled and left the plane.

I was not feeling sick anymore, and I had no fear since my mind had been focused on the Lord. I opened up Renee's other two letters to read while waiting to disembark. At the very end of the last letter, Renee wrote, "Tell the lady next to you that I will be praying for her"

A chill went up my spine, and I couldn't wait to ask Renee what was in that letter I had given her.

At home, I called Renee and asked her what she had written in that letter. She said, "That was the one with the gospel tract in it." Then Renee said excitedly, "I wrote, 'Dear Susanne, the lady sitting to your left needs to know Jesus.'"

The faithfulness of a few people set up a divine appointment. I don't know if Cathy responded to God's message, but God showed me that He knows exactly where I am and who is with me at all times. I never need to be afraid.

Author Bio

Susanne Horn lives with her husband, Joel, and their three children, Hannah, Josiah, and Benjamin, in St. Paul, Minnesota. She enjoys home schooling her children, and while she still doesn't like to fly, she does fly several times a year.

GOD IS SO GOOD!

Tom Houck

I should have driven to the hospital the previous night, but I wanted to cross off as many items as possible on my to-do list before leaving town. I figured it would be fine to drive to Pennsylvania the following morning.

It was the spring of 2001, and my 75-year-old father needed two stents in his heart. The operation was to be performed in Hershey, Pennsylvania, about two hours from my parents' home in State College. My wife and I lived in Northern Virginia, roughly two hours in the opposite direction from the medical center.

The surgery was scheduled for Thursday morning, but Dad was admitted the night before. This meant that my mother would stay in a nearby hotel. Meanwhile, I planned to drive up Thursday morning and hopefully arrive before the surgery began. It seemed like a good plan after the doctors told us that this type of procedure was routine.

But I started feeling uneasy on Wednesday night. Mom called after checking into the hotel, and she seemed to be scared. Not only was she concerned about Dad's pending surgery, but she is legally blind and was staying in a hotel by herself for the first time in her life—a fact that I previously did not know!

I immediately regretted my decision to leave the following morning. I should have been with my mother, instead of worrying about a to-do list. In this moment of guilt, I suddenly realized that my behavior wasn't anything new. I often put my own needs in front of others.' When people needed help, I often had commitments that I could not do anything about. But now, the image of my scared and near-blind mother in a strange hotel room brought me to my knees. "Dear God," I prayed, "Please forgive my selfishness. Help me to change my natural tendencies."

After tossing and turning much of the night, morning finally arrived. My wife, Kim, and I were delayed and got a late start to Hershey. Then, heavy traffic slowed us down even more. With the previous night's guilt fresh on my mind, I started worrying that I might not see Dad before the operation. And then I imagined the worst. *What if something goes wrong?* What if I never saw Dad alive again?

Even though I had asked God for forgiveness the previous night, I wondered if this might be punishment for my selfishness. I feared that I was in store for a painful lesson that wouldn't be forgotten for a long time. In reality, I didn't appreciate the nature of God's forgiveness.

We arrived in Hershey, and Dad was still waiting to be called for surgery. *Whew!* The surgeon appeared and explained that the operation would last about an hour, and we wished Dad good luck.

The hour passed relatively quickly, but there was no sign of Dad. As each minute rolled by, the clock seemed to move slower. Eighty, one hundred, one hundred and twenty minutes. What in the world was happening?

One hundred forty, one sixty, one seventy-five...three hours had elapsed! Obviously, there were complications. I suddenly remembered that our neighbor's husband unexpectedly died on the operating table at this very same hospital! I fully expected a somber-faced surgeon to enter our room at any time.

Finally, I heard some commotion. I moved toward the hallway and was the first to catch a glimpse of Dad's bed being pushed in our direction. "Here comes Dad," I remember yelling to Mom and Kim. He was awake!

For a brief instant, I was transplanted back to my childhood. No longer was I a grown man, but rather a little boy thrilled to see his daddy. From my perch at the front window, I saw him coming home from work as I excitedly yelled, "Daddy's home!"

I snapped back to reality. We soon learned that although the procedure was long, it was successful. Unfortunately, Dad wasn't out of the woods. Partially because he was diabetic, Dad experienced a variety of problems in the subsequent days, remaining hospitalized much longer than anyone expected.

During this difficult time, I stayed in Hershey with my mother while Kim returned to Virginia. She was six months pregnant at the time, and I wanted her to rest. Meanwhile, I became convinced that Dad was going to die. His condition was not improving, and the doctors were unable to explain anything.

For the first time, I realized my parents wouldn't live forever. It was especially difficult because I knew Dad would never see my first child. And I so desperately wanted this great and decent man to hold our baby.

I cried and prayed to God a zillion times during this period. And guess what? God answered our prayers! Dad's condition slowly improved, and within a few months, he seemed like his old self again.

That summer, Kim gave birth to our first child, Matthew Paul two weeks before he was due. Ten days later, my parents arrived in town to spend a week with us. I thought this day would never happen. So when Dad finally held our tiny newborn, I thanked God again for being so good to our family. And I took lots of videos and photographs!

Nine days after returning to Pennsylvania, Dad died of a sudden heart attack. It was unexpected and tragic, but the timing made me realize even more how God had blessed us. He healed my father in Hershey and allowed him to live just long enough to hold our first child. Was it a fluke that Matthew was born two weeks before his due date? I don't think so. If he had been born when originally expected, my Dad would probably have never seen him.

But the beauty of God's plan didn't end there. Our baby brought joy and laughter to a grieving grandmother who desperately missed her husband of 54 years. Although she was legally blind and suddenly lonely, God's gift of a healthy, little boy brought her happiness in the difficult months and years to come. What a wonderful way to help a widow deal with a heartbreaking loss.

When naming our son, we chose the name Paul for his middle name in honor of my Dad. But we selected Matthew because it was the only boy's name that Kim and I could agree upon! Ironically, his first name seemed incredibly fitting in light of these events. Matthew means "Gift from God."

As I later reflected on God's workings in our lives, I recalled my pledge to help other people instead of constantly tending to my own agenda. I remembered how God could have chastised me, but He chose to overwhelm me with blessings. Not only did He give me the greatest gift in history when Jesus died on a cross, but I learned about His constant and incredible love for His children while they live on this earth.

As Psalm 145:9 (NIV) says, *"The Lord is good to all; he has compassion on all he has made."* More than ever, I know this is true!

Author Bio

Tom Houck lives in Ashburn, Virginia with his wife, Kim and son, Matthew. He recently completed writing his first book about the Bible. Tom enjoys playing and composing songs on the piano, playing "electric football" and spending time with his family.

FINDING COMFORT IN AN
UNCOMFORTABLE PLACE

Kelly Kauffman

My hands were trembling as I reached for the directions in my travel bag. "When you arrive in Albuquerque, call the hotel hotline printed at the bottom of this page. The hotel will send a free shuttle to the airport and take you to your hotel. Reservations have already been made in your name."

OK...find a phone...don't look scared...I'm here because this is where God wants me to be, right? I had never been so far from home, completely alone. It was the summer between my sophomore and junior years of college, and I was more than a thousand miles from my home in central Illinois. I had been sent to the Navajo Reservation for the summer to work with Baptist Churches doing Vacation Bible School and other summer programs.

As I found the payphone, my shaking fingers dialed the number and I asked for a shuttle. I was told it would take about a half-hour for the shuttle to arrive. I dragged all of my luggage out to the side-walk and sat atop my largest suitcase. Waiting for my shuttle was the longest thirty minutes of my life as I sat contemplating how I found myself in this position in the first place.

Earlier that year, a couple of college-aged women came to the Baptist Student Union, which I belonged to on my college campus; they talked about their experiences on a summer mission trip to Mexico. While they were talking, I felt a strong pull on my heart to do the same. With the help of my mother, I found information on applying for a summer missionary position and completed all the necessary paperwork. A few months later, I was standing in the airport in St. Louis with plane tickets to Albuquerque, New Mexico. I did not know very much about the Navajo Indian culture, but I knew that I was supposed to find out first hand.

However, once I found myself sitting on the sidewalk outside of the Albuquerque airport waiting for a shuttle, I began questioning whether or not God really meant to send me here. I'd never been to Albuquerque, much less the Navajo Nation. I was alone and wasn't going to meet my partner for another twenty-four hours. For the first time traveling by myself to an unknown city, I felt a loneliness I'd never experienced.

Already fighting tears of homesickness, I looked up and saw a white van with the hotel logo painted across the side. It pulled up to the sidewalk, and the driver saw me and helped lug my bags into the van. As I began sliding open the back door he stopped me. "You're my only passenger this time. You're more than welcome to sit up front. It's cooler up here."

"Okay," I replied hesitantly. I wanted to sit in the back and be left alone so I could further list the reasons I should still be in Illinois, but I did not want to seem rude so I pulled myself up into the front seat of the van.

"Boy, you sure do have an awful lot of luggage for just one person. How long are you here for?" the driver asked me.

"All summer," I said out loud wishing he hadn't reminded me of that.

"Wow! You got relatives nearby or something?"

"No, actually my family is back in Illinois. I'm going to the Navajo Nation to work with their children on a summer mission trip," I answered.

"No kidding! That is so cool! Are you here alone?"

"I'll have a partner, but she won't get here until tomorrow."

"I see. Well, I know you are probably scared. You're far away from home and going to an unfamiliar area with a completely different culture." *He read my mind*, I thought. *Am I that transparent?*

"I am a cop full-time. I drive this shuttle part-time on my days off. And I am a pretty new Christian. Being a police officer can be pretty scary. But I've been learning verses from the Bible, and I want to share one with you that I use when I'm scared. It's Philippians 4:13 (NKJV), *'I can do all things through Christ who strengthens me.'* I tell myself that verse, and I remind myself that it says all things, not only the easy things that we do."

I was speechless. Through that short conversation, my whole attitude changed. My doubt was gone. I was able to remember how excited I'd felt when I applied for the summer missionary position. I was able to feel God's presence and reassurance as I rode through the unfamiliar streets of Albuquerque. And, amazingly, I knew that throughout the whole summer I would be confronted with unfamiliar situations, but I felt a peace. I knew that with Christ's strength, I would get through all of them.

I don't know how many times I repeated Philippians 4:13 to myself throughout that summer and in the days since then. It has been my favorite Bible verse since that day, and I have relied on it through many different struggles. That man in the shuttle was put in my life at that very moment to help restore my faith in my heavenly Father who gives me the strength to get through all of life's challenges.

—————————— AUTHOR BIO ——————————

Mrs. Kauffman lives in Indiana with her husband, Aaron. She enjoys working and playing with children, including eleven nephews and nieces.

SOMETIMES GOD WEARS SKIN

Christine Kozlowski

At times God seems as far away as the deepest recesses of space. My head tells me God is listening but my heart feels like He's left me on hold. It is in these moments that I wish that God could wear skin.

I've since observed that sometimes God does wear skin. He often uses people I would least expect to make His presence known.

My morning prayer time was once again dry. I had always had the ability to see God in the ordinary, and I lamented to Him that morning that I'd like to see Him in my day. I needed to know He was real. I set off for work that morning praying that God would answer my small prayer.

Tears streamed down Elizabeth's face as she entered the office telling me she was hurt. I asked the kindergartner where she was hurt and she pointed to her heart.

As an elementary school secretary, I've seen my fare share of scrapes and broken bones. However, I'd never encountered a child so young with a heart problem. Usually parents will give us details about their child's medical condition. I knew Elizabeth's medical records showed nothing unusual. Elizabeth was one of our homeless students. Although her mother could pay a monthly rent, she didn't have the funds for a security deposit. Many of our homeless families found it less expensive to live in a hotel where they only had to pay a monthly fee.

I calmed her down with soothing words, and the tears stopped flowing as she told me her story. It seems she wanted to hug a classmate but the child rejected her hug, pushing her away. Elizabeth's pain was real and I wondered how I could heal her wounded heart. Silently, I sent God a small plea for some help. Elizabeth needed to know that she was loved and that she was special. I told her some people just didn't like hugging, but if it would make her feel better, she could give me a hug.

In today's world, hugging a student can be misread. As school employees, we are told that the least amount of physical contact is the best. I observed that there was another adult nearby. Knowing full well that I could come under fire for the small kindness of a hug, I gathered my courage together and hoped my actions would ease Elizabeth's broken heart.

I bent down to eye level with her, and she threw her tiny little arms around my neck. I hugged her to me and smiled as I released her. Quick as a wink, she kissed my cheek, smiled from ear to ear and set off skipping towards her classroom.

At that moment I knew God had answered my morning prayer, and perhaps I gained more that day than she did. As I gave her my outward sign of love, I knew those little arms surrounding me were God's. Deep within, I felt His immense love warm my parched spirit.

God wasn't light years away. On that day, God reached out to me in the skin of a kindergartner. All it took on my part was an unexpected hug, and her tiny kiss on the cheek broke through my dried spirit. In that small kiss, God's love flooded me with warmth, and I felt revived. God does indeed wear skin. I only had to discover Him in the packaging.

─── AUTHOR BIO ───

Chris Kozlowski lives in Sterling Heights, Michigan with her husband Ron. Employed as an elementary school secretary, she is also active in her church, St. Blase. Besides writing a weekly column for the church bulletin, she also sings with one of the church choirs, the contemporary group, Remnant.

I Am Free

Joseph A. Mantini

A Plea for Help

Born into an abusive and alcoholic environment, I viewed that world as normal, so my lifestyle was already etched in stone. In my teenage years, drugs, domestic violence, and drinking was my life. Selling drugs, which almost ended my life, was my way of financing my drug needs. I couldn't hold a job because the cocaine clouded my mind. I had two marriages that fell apart due to my abusive actions toward my wives.

I stopped using hard drugs at age thirty-four, but continued to smoke marijuana. After an MRI test, my brain showed lots of tissue damage that could never be repaired. It was then that I decided my life was over. I attempted suicide, twice. And I was trying the third time when I heard the voice of God say, "No! I have something better for you."

A Positive Message

Then I heard the good news of Jesus Christ. God sent a man into my life who helped me with my walk. I called his church and he told me "come as you are." I have never forgotten those words. Today he is my pastor and best friend. His Biblical teachings have guided me through the Bible to discover answers to difficult problems and have given me strength when I wanted to give up. He taught me how to pray and showed me the real Jesus Christ.

Giving Thanks

My life is not perfect, but all the bad habits in my life are gone. I have numerous health problems from my former lifestyle. I have a disability that causes pain daily. All of this is a reminder of how my life was before I turned to the Lord.

God has sent me a wife; we have been married five years, and she has allowed the Lord to work in her life also. We attend church, read the Bible, teach Bible studies, and work together in a community outreach ministry at the local Rescue Mission for Men & Women.

I found real freedom in my life, only after I turned it over to God.

AUTHOR BIO

Joseph Mantini lives in Pueblo, Colorado with his wife, Mary. He started a community outreach in July 2002 called J.C. Ministries (helping people discover the real Jesus Christ). He speaks monthly at the local Rescue Mission sharing the Word of God and his personal testimony.

A SUBTLE HINT

Rick Martin

January, 1960
Greenwich Village
New York City, New York

The frozen streets of the "city that never sleeps" are barely manageable. The snow is falling lightly, but the wind is blowing cold, and the ice is very slick. As the cab slowly makes its way to the entrance of St. Vincent's Hospital, Richard and Elsie Martin are calm and collected. This is, after all, their third child, and they have been through this before. On January 23rd, 1960, at 2:15 am, I am born.

Summer, 1968
LaPuente, California

I am eight years old now, and we are visiting relatives out west. I love the large cement pool in the backyard! When the other kids are all dried off and inside watching television, I'm still in the water. I'm a good swimmer and am becoming a bit of a daredevil on the low diving board. My cousin Bobby, a freshman in college, is on the roof sunning, and I am alone in the pool. I attempt what I think is another perfect back flip when the back of my head crashes into the diving board.

When I open my eyes, I am lying face up at the bottom of the pool. It is so calm and so serene. I can see the rays of the sun, shining like a beacon through the crystal blue water. I am breathing easily. Long, deep breaths. It is the greatest feeling I have ever known up until this point in my life. On this warm summer day in 1968, I have died.

The splash was huge, as Bobby dove off of the roof and into the water. He scooped me up like a shortstop picks up a routine grounder and got me out of the pool. Later, as I sat on the lounge chair in a towel, someone said to me, "Boy, you are one lucky guy! We thought we lost you for good. Someone's looking out for you, I can tell you that!" I didn't know what that meant. I didn't get it. All I knew then was that I wanted a peanut butter and jelly sandwich, and I wanted to go back in the pool. I got the sandwich.

Spring 1977
Clifton, New Jersey.

It's unusually warm for this time of year. I am riding the bus, and it is so warm that the driver has the door and all of the windows open. Maybe the air conditioner was not working? I ring the bar to signal my stop, and as the bus slows, I make my way up the aisle. As I approach the top of the stairs leading to the exit door, the bus suddenly stops, and I am launched down the stairs! I can see the shiny metal door guards staring me in the eye and I duck! Crash! The top of my head smacks straight into the metal guard and I roll out of the bus into the street. My head is bleeding and the blood is running into my eyes.

I lie on my back and clear the blood from my eyes. As I lie there staring up at the sky, I can see rays of sunlight, shining through the clouds like a beacon. I am breathing easily. Long, deep breaths. It is the greatest feeling I have ever known up until this point in my life. On this warm spring day in 1977, I have died. Again.

I awake in a hospital room. One hundred and eighty-seven stitches and a major headache later, I am still stunned. A nurse comes over to see me and says "You are one lucky young man. Thought we lost you there for a minute!" She laughs softly and says "Somebody was certainly looking out for you today." I don't know what that means. I don't get it. All I know is I want a peanut butter and jelly sandwich, and I want to go back to school. I get the sandwich first.

January 1987
Largo, Florida.

The apartment is cold, and my wife asks me to close the wall vent so it does not blow the cold air on her. It's a short leap for me to pull the lever down. I jump and slap at the lever with my left hand. My hand hits it hard and my wedding band wraps tightly around the lever. The sound of bone breaking and flesh tearing is unlike anything I have ever heard.

My ring finger is ripped from my body and I am in agony. I am taken to a local hospital where the surgeon informs me that I will be awake for the surgery as he attempts to save whatever is left of my finger. In the Operating Room, the technician tells me he will be giving me a nerve block. This will numb all of the nerves in my arm before the surgery. As soon as he injects the needle, I know something is wrong. My head feels like it is exploding, and I can hear myself scream.

Suddenly I am lying on my back. The pain is gone and I can see the bright lights of the operating room flood lamps shining on me like a beacon. I am breathing easily. Long, deep breaths. It is the greatest feeling I have ever known up until this point in my life. On this sunny winter day in 1987, I have died. Again!

I awake in a hospital room, nauseous and dizzy. The needle I was given missed the nerve and hit an artery, stopping my heart. The surgeon says I am very lucky to be around. He says someone had my back last night in that room. I don't know what that means. I don't get it. All I know is I want a peanut butter and jelly sandwich, and I want to go home. I get the sandwich first.

Summer 1991
Clearwater, Florida

I arrived at the hospital for some x-rays that my doctor wanted. They would inject a red dye into my system and take pictures. It didn't sound like a big deal. They asked if I had ever had this done before, and I admitted that I had not. As I sat on the gurney, the injection felt warm. Then hot. Then hotter! My head felt like it was exploding and I can hear myself scream. I hear someone yell, "Code 99!"

Suddenly I am lying on my back. The pain is gone and I can see the bright lights of the x-ray room flood lamps shining on me like a beacon. I am breathing easily. Long, deep breaths. It was the greatest feeling I had ever known up until that point in my life. On this hot summer day in 1991, I have died. AGAIN!

I awaken in the x-ray room, shaken and scared. The technician marvels at how lucky I am. "Yeah, I know." I sigh. "Someone is looking out for me right?" "You bet they are," he replies. I still don't know what that means. I still don't get it. All I know is I want a peanut butter and jelly sandwich and I want to go home. I get the sandwich and then go home.

June 2001
First United Methodist Church
Pinellas Park, Florida

I nervously stand there with my wife at my side. In a moment, my life will change forever. Pastor John Barham emerges with a small bottle of water in his hands. Water brought back from the River Jordan in Israel. As he baptizes me, I gaze over his shoulder. The rays of sunlight passing through the large stained glass window behind him shine like a beacon. I am breathing easily. Long, deep breaths. It still is the greatest feeling I had ever known in my life. On a beautiful June day in 2001, I am born. Again.

After the service my pastor tells me how blessed I am. How someone is looking out for me. How someone loves me. And I get it. Somehow after all of this time, I finally understand who was watching over me. As I drive home that day, my hunger is great. I hunger for more knowledge, I hunger for more spirituality, and I hunger for the forgiveness and the love of Jesus Christ. And for the first time in my life, I don't have the slightest urge for a peanut butter and jelly sandwich.

──────── AUTHOR BIO ────────
Rick Martin lives in Florida with his wife, Gail, of twenty years and their dogs and cats. Rick loves his Lord Jesus Christ, his family, his church, and the occassional peanut butter and jelly sandwich.

THE TALE OF THE MISSING PURSE

Phil Nicholas

Last year I drove my daughter from our home in Miami to college in Charleston, South Carolina, which is a good eight-hour drive up I-95. We loaded everything in the car and stopped along the way several times for gas, food, rest stops, and finally made it to our destination.

At some point, my daughter came into the room of her new apartment crying "Dad, I can't find my purse!"

"Well," I responded, "it has to be around here." But after two hours of searching, and after my "Please God" prayer, we could not find the purse.

Now, this was no ordinary purse. It had several hundred dollars in it, along with all of my daughter's I.D., everything she needed to transfer her life from Florida to South Carolina. She had her passport in a separate suitcase, and I dished out the several hundred dollars needed for the first month's rent, electric, and some spending money! But hey, it was my daughter!

We forgot about the lost purse and decided just to enjoy our time together. I stayed the night, and the next day I took my daughter and her roommate out to explore Charleston. Around 4:00 p.m., it was time for me to leave. Kissing my daughter goodbye, I started back down that six hundred-mile stretch of I-95 toward Miami.

About three hours into my drive, while listening to the Super Bowl, I got an overwhelming craving for a Dairy Queen Oreo Blizzard. I had not had one of these amazing concoctions in several months. But I knew, sitting there, driving in the dark, that I HAD TO HAVE ONE! So, I looked for those exit signs you normally see just before a highway exit that tell you what restaurants, gas stations, etc. are coming up. I saw a sign with a Dairy Queen logo, but I did not need gas just yet, so I figured I would wait until I did need gas before

I pulled off the highway. After several miles, another exit sign with a Dairy Queen logo came into view, but I still did not need gas. Finally, after several more miles I realized that it would be forever before I needed gas, so I resolved to stop at the next Dairy Queen exit.

Driving along, I spotted an exit coming up ahead, but I did not see a Dairy Queen logo on the exit signage. *Oh well*, I thought. Then suddenly, to my left, in the middle of the median, I saw a huge sign in bold letters "DAIRY QUEEN, EXIT NOW, TURN LEFT."

Startled, I immediately got into the exit lane to find that Dairy Queen! At the bottom of the ramp, I turned left, but I did not see a Dairy Queen in sight. However, I did see a Burger King, but there was something unusual. *Why?* I said to myself. *Is that the Burger King Jenifer and I stopped at on the way up here?* Then I saw a convenience store across the street, and remembered that we did indeed stop at a convenience store on the way up. Suddenly, with chills coming up my spine, I exclaimed, "Lord, are you directing me to find my daughter's purse?"

It could not be, but I pulled into the lot. Mine was the only car there and I was the only person in the store, other than the six-ear-ringed young man who was washing windows.

"Excuse me, but I think my daughter and I were up here yesterday. She lost her purse. Did you find a purse?"

The young man responded, "Where's she from?" A bit startled by the question, I said, "Er...Pembroke Pines, Florida." The man simply responded, "Yep, we got that purse. Lot of money in that purse." He then handed me a business card saying, "Here is the sheriff's number; case number is on the back. Give him a call. He's got your purse."

I could have passed out right there. I just took the card from the young man, and in a state of shock and disbelief, I mumbled, "Thank you."

I made my way to my car in a daze. *Wow!* "Thank you, Father." We got that purse back, money and all!

I never did find that Dairy Queen. But I found one down the road, and had the best Diary Queen Oreo Blizzard that I have ever had, knowing that my heavenly Father really does care about the details of our lives!

AUTHOR BIO

Phil Nicholas is an attorney in Miami, working for
Amadeus North America, LLC. A devoted husband and
father, he has been a Christian for 11 years. His home
church is Christ Covenant Presbyterian in Davie.

MY TURKEY BUZZARDS

Renee Ortiz

It was early spring when I was finally able to go to our church's women's retreat. I had wanted to go the past few years, but stayed behind to teach children's church, take care of my kids, and for every other reason I could think of.

I love working with the kids at our church; I teach Sunday school and the midweek program, but when it comes to being with the grown-ups, I get a bit shy. So my prayer for this weekend was, "Please, Dear Lord, let me reach out to other women. Help me to get past my shyness and help someone."

It was a beautiful retreat; it was everything I imagined and more. The setting was spectacular: we sang to God in a ministry center that looked out at a forest of redwoods. The weather was perfect. The speaker was inspiring. We even had secret sisters, whom we would pray for during the weekend and write anonymous notes of encouragement to. At the Sunday brunch, our identities would be revealed.

Which brings me to my first stumbling block of the weekend. There were 150 women, and I had no idea which one was my secret sister. I wrote notes to her, nevertheless, and prayed and scanned the nametags whenever I could, but I couldn't find her.

On Saturday morning we had a time to go off in the woods with a Bible and journal and a list of questions to spend some real quality time with God. It was an incredible roller coaster of prayers and praises. Being a mom, there isn't often the time to just break down and cry with God; there would be too many questions from family members and friends. But cry I did, and I felt so loved by Our Father. Time got away, and too soon, I had to head back to join the others for lunch.

On the hike back, I pulled out my binoculars and asked God to show me a cool bird. I had been searching earlier with no luck. Wouldn't you know it? Out of nowhere swept in four turkey buzzards. Granted, they're anything but beautiful, though their sheer immensity is awe-inspiring. They did this perfect loop and disappeared. I don't have to tell you how big my smile was as I nearly skipped the rest of the way back!

Jumping to stumbling block number two of the weekend. I was going to have to go back home early on Sunday. I was leading the children's musical and had to be back for the first rehearsal. I figured if I left right after the Sunday service, I would make it just in time. So I'd miss the brunch. At least I had most of the weekend. Besides, I was sure this was God's plan.

My first problem was that I still didn't know my secret sister. I hated to leave without meeting her. Secondly, I didn't want to admit it, but I really hadn't reached out like I had hoped. I did talk to many of the women. I participated, but I didn't feel as though my prayer had been answered. Thirdly, the pastor spoke too long! Don't get me wrong, it was wonderful! But I was late! And then, as I was racing out the door, I finally met my secret sister.

We hugged, and then I ran to my car and proceeded to high-tail it out of there. I had to get back for the kids. I prayed as I drove and even though there was some strange red light flashing on my dashboard, I said, "God, this is what you wanted, right?"

I started to take the curves a bit fast and then slowed down and prayed some more, "Lord, I'll make it on time, right?" I looked up then, and you won't believe what I saw! Four turkey buzzards swooped down out of nowhere, did a loop, and took off. It was a sign! And while I was looking at that sign, I missed the sign that told me where to turn, and before too long, I realized I was heading in the wrong direction. Now I was really late!

"What's the deal, God? This is what You wanted." I put on my turn signal, and slowed to turn around. The car behind me slowed as well. The car behind him didn't. CRASH! I have never been in a car accident before. I've never even seen one, which is surprising because I grew up in Southern California! My car didn't get touched. The other two had bumped up fenders and broken lights. It really wasn't too bad, but there was a shaken up little girl whom I felt bad for.

After I saw that all was okay, I was shaking. I knew I needed to go back to the retreat. The hope of getting to the rehearsal was long past, and maybe I could still catch the end of the brunch. Most of the women were gone by the time I got back. There were a few still there taking things down, packing up. I wasn't sure what I needed, but was overcome with a tremendous desire to visit the tiny chapel. It was a beautiful candlelit room in the middle of the trees. I went in, and there kneeling at the altar and crying to our God, was my secret sister.

I went to her, and we talked and prayed. I had been through some similar things that she was going through, and God filled me with words of encouragement for her. We hugged and she eventually went on her way.

I went outside, and took a seat by a waterfall to catch my breath. Was it possible that God used a minor fender bender to grab my attention? I rejoiced that God had been able to use me. I thanked Him for answering my prayer as well, and I praised Him for being so awesome! And as I did, I looked up. Four turkey buzzards swooped down, did a loop and disappeared. I will never again be able to look at those magnificent, hideous birds without a word of thanks to God.

AUTHOR BIO

Renee Ortiz resides in Windsor, California, with her husband, Patrick, three children, Patrick II, Jonah, and Madeline, and an incredibly large pile of laundry. She home-schools, leads a den of Cub Scouts and teaches children's church, a midweek kid's program, and directs her church's musical.

TRUTH IN OUR CRAZY WORLD

Amanda Denise Osberg

I've spent my whole life wishing I were someone or something else. I gaze at people's appearances and comment on how gorgeous or perfect they look, yet judge myself with disdain and mock my slightest imperfection. I claim to have child-like faith, yet question God's intentions and motives for my life. *Does God really have a plan for me?* The fact of the matter is, I live in a backward world where morals no longer matter, but appearances and doubts overtake everything I thought was important.

According to society, I'm too much of a person by about fifty pounds. I'm awkward and weird because I've never been on a date or shared a first kiss. I stand out as odd because I wear clothes that actually cover my body. I don't cuss, drink, or do drugs, and am in favor of abstinence. Society frowns upon my behavior.

In order to cure people like me, society throws vulgar music and immoral movies at me in order to suck me into their sense of normalcy and happiness. Women who wear a size zero and men with big muscles and six-packs are intended to portray the image of an ideal American and, therefore, are envied.

I begin to watch them, study their lifestyle, and become dissatisfied or disgusted with myself. I go on countless diets, change my wardrobe, dye my hair, and purchase worthless objects all to take on a star's identity. I'm no longer myself, but a creature vaguely resembling someone familiar. I've been snared in society's trap, always wishing to become someone I can never be. If I become someone I don't recognize anymore, then society has won.

Finally, I see how stupid my actions and thoughts are, for I already have the attention of the greatest Someone in the entire universe. I am important, and I don't need to change who I am to feel as if I fit in. The Lord Almighty has created me, and He doesn't want me to fit in. I am called to lead a different life and stand out as an alien in this crazy world. And you know what? God doesn't make mistakes.

But, not only was I created to be different, I was made for a reason. God didn't just dump me on this planet and leave me to fend for myself. He has a specific plan for my life. I may feel unimportant, but I couldn't be more wrong. If I make a difference in only one person's life the whole time I'm on earth, that would be enough. My life will have been worth living.

I was specially created by God Himself to live one life—mine. God sculpted me the way He saw fit. He knew what I would look like and doesn't want me any different. He created me to carry out a special task. He has a plan for my life, and I need to trust that He'll carry it out in His time. I am made perfect in every aspect, through the Father's eyes.

AUTHOR BIO

Amanda Osberg, a junior at Westminster Academy, enjoys reading and writing stories. Her goal in high school is to make a positive impact in the lives of as many people as possible. She has carried this out through leading Bible studies, worship services, and striving to live a life worthy of Christ.

TELLING GOD WHAT TO DO

Tina Patete

Never tell God what to do. That seems like a simple command, easy enough to follow. Not if you're me, a twenty-two-year-old college Junior. At least I was, five years ago. I accepted Christ at the ripe old age of four. I'm a crawl-down-the-aisle Christian. My mother shared her strong faith with me from the very beginning of my life. I have two younger sisters, and the four of us lived in subsidized housing in a small town in Pennsylvania.

I could write this entire story about how poor we were and about how God continually and miraculously met all of our needs. There are many examples of how the exact amount of money we needed to turn our water back on would arrive in the mail from some kind-hearted soul. As wonderfully uplifting as those stories are, there is a greater story even still that I would like to tell. It is the story of how God changed my life and I came to know Him in a greater way than I ever could have imagined.

My mother had surgery for a benign brain tumor when I was a senior in high school. Even after the removal of the tumor and the long healing process, she was never quite the same. She just never seemed to get better. She had numerous doctors' visits and sometimes a different diagnosis with each one.

Then it happened. The day I told God what to do. Actually, I told Him what not to do. I was away at college and my mother was having surgery for one of the aforementioned diagnoses. I would normally have been there for the procedure, but I had been to all of her previous surgeries, and this one was during the week of finals. She told me it was outpatient surgery and was not a big deal. So there I was, doing my laundry Friday morning when it was time for her surgery. As I stood in front of the washing machine, I looked toward the heavens and challenged my Heavenly Father with this, "Lord, You can't take her today because I just can't handle it, okay?"

Feeling that my request was heard and obviously going to be granted, I studied the rest of the day and went to bed. Then the beeping and the yelling began Saturday morning. I struggled out of bed, only to go downstairs to the sound of my little sister's voice screaming from the answering machine for me to pick up while an operator was asking me to accept the call. I picked up the phone and accepted the charges as my sister informed me that my beloved mother was dead.

"You're lying!" I screamed. "Shut up, Bridget! Stop saying that!" Then the paramedic took the phone from her and uttered the words that changed my life, "Ma'am, ma'am, this is the paramedic. Yes, your mother has passed away."

I threw the phone as hard as I could. DIDN'T YOU HEAR ME, GOD? I CAN'T HANDLE THIS RIGHT NOW!

When I arrived home, there was a blur of people and phone calls and hugs and tears. It was decided that my sisters and I would stay with an elder of our church and his family. The girls were extremely traumatized after finding my mother that morning. She had died in her sleep from an illness completely unrelated to the surgery and amazingly, never diagnosed. There were funeral arrangements to make, our apartment needed to be cleaned out and there were legal matters. My sisters were under age. One was 16 and the other was only 12. I had every intention of taking full responsibility for them and said so without hesitation.

As the day continued, I had a lot of visitors. Many people prayed for me and with me. But I was still numb. I had so much pain. It was so deep and so sharp and like nothing I had ever felt before. My best friend in the all of the world was gone! My mother was like no other woman. She had faced so many trials and terrors in her life and yet she had never turned her back on God. She had raised three children without a husband or a steady income. She never blamed God when we had to eat macaroni and cheese every day for a week. She praised Him and taught us to do the same. She was the reason I was working so hard. Her faith was unmatched among all of the women I had met. She knew the Bible through and through. She LIVED for Christ.

That night, God gave me the verse. The one I will never forget. The one I have engraved on my heart. *"...to live is Christ and to die is gain."* (Philippians 1:21b, NIV)

That night I confessed my sin to God Almighty. That night I thanked Him for taking away all of her pain. She would never be sick again. She would never cry out in the middle of the hallway, too weak to take another step. There would be no more ambulances when she couldn't breathe in the middle of church. There would be no more trying to find a ride to drive us forty-five minutes to the doctor's office. Now she was in Heaven. The only place she ever wanted to go. She had never seen the beach, never been out of the country, and never bought herself a brand new shirt.

She was finally home. That night I understood all of that, accepted it. I gave my burden of grief to my Savior and thanked Him for making all things work together for good.

What happened next was astonishing. There was the matter of the bill for the funeral. The church asked for donations instead of flowers. We received more than enough to pay for the funeral. There were donations from several churches and people of the community. We moved into the apartment in our chapel that was used for visiting missionaries. In the months to follow, my two sisters and I moved back to Messiah College so that I could finish my senior year. The college allowed us to live on campus in married housing. They also gathered food from the students and provided us with so many bins we ended up giving some away! Someone even paid for my youngest sister to attend a Christian school. That had been one of my mother's daily prayers.

My life completely changed that year. God took from me the one person that meant everything in the world to me, but He brought me to a deeper commitment to Him. I learned that His yoke was easy and His burden was light. I learned that He would *never* leave me nor forsake me. It has been five years since my mother's death. I am now married and have a son. My youngest sister continues to live with us and will be a senior at a Christian school. I still miss my mother a lot, but I think about the day she met her Heavenly Father and I can almost hear Him saying, "Welcome Home."

AUTHOR BIO

Tina Patete is an elementary school teacher for
Great Commission School in Altoona, Pennsylvania.
She resides with her husband, Douglas, her sister,
Salina, and her son, Logan Christopher.

ARRESTED BY GOD'S LOVE

Penny Phagan
as told by Lance Phagan

I pushed the door open to the convenience store. At the sound of
the bell, several people looked up as I entered. Something did not feel
right. "Give me a pack of Marlboro Lights," I said to the clerk behind
the counter. I laid my money down on the counter, picked up my
cigarettes and walked out. I looked around and saw my customer
standing beside the phone booth where we had agreed to meet.
I fingered the eight ball of crank in my pocket. I had sold drugs to
him before, so I expected this to be a fairly routine drug sale. I looked
around and saw that a couple of the customers had exited the
convenience store behind me. I started walking across the parking
lot to the designated meeting place.

"Freeze! Police! Put your hands on your head and get down on
the ground!"

I felt the cold steel of the gun against the back of my neck.
Suddenly, I was surrounded by six undercover police officers. One
searched me for weapons and took the knife I wore in a sheath on
my belt. He also found the eight ball of crank I was carrying. I was
handcuffed and put into the back of an unmarked police car. Several
of the officers began to search my truck for more drugs. I had been on
a three day drug-induced high, but I knew enough to realize I was in
big trouble.

My customer turned out to be an undercover policeman. My
friend, Doc, had introduced me to him. I later found out that Doc had
turned in several people, including me, in order to reduce his own
drug trafficking charge and avoid time in jail.

After being questioned for about thirty minutes, I was turned over
to a uniformed policeman and taken to Cobb County Detention
Center for booking. At the jail, I was placed in a holding cell.

Conditions were crowded. I waited about an hour before I was called out and fingerprinted. Next, I was processed and placed into the regular jail population. In times past, I had called my mother or other relatives and they bailed me out. But this time, I did not have any more chances. I was already on two years probation for possession of marijuana, so I was unable to post bond. There was no way out this time.

After about five weeks in jail, I began to visit the prison chaplain, Chaplain Hutchinson, to talk with him about my mother's health problems. I was really worried about her and hoped he could check in on her for me. Hutch, as he was affectionately called, began to encourage me to read the Bible and several other Christian books he gave to me.

On November 30, 1995, I prayed the sinner's prayer with Chaplain Hutch and received Jesus as my Savior. I had been arrested on possession of a controlled substance, but in reality, God had used this situation to arrest me with His love. I had been chasing a high for most of my adult life through drugs and alcohol. I had destroyed my family and many other relationships that were dear to me. But God, in His mercy, saw that I needed a Savior. He used what the enemy meant for destruction in my life as a means of getting my attention. What some people may term the worst thing that could happen, actually turned out for my good. It was only after I was arrested and put in prison that I discovered God's love and freedom from the sin that had gripped my life for so many years.

After being released from prison, God led me to a church where I could use my talents for Him. I play bass on our church worship team, and I am the men's fellowship coordinator. He has also blessed me with a wonderful wife and child. God has truly arrested me with His love, and, like Paul, I can say that I am a bondservant of Jesus Christ.

──── AUTHOR BIO ────

Penny Phagan lives in Stockbridge, Georgia with her husband, Lance and son, Joshua. She is involved with the marketing department at her local church and attends the MOPS of Faith group in her area. Penny enjoys reading, writing, singing, and spending time with her family.

WALKING THROUGH SORROW

Cindy Pocapalia

Sometimes we have to walk through pain, and sorrow in order for God to prove His love for us. The journey is difficult, but at the end, there is joy. I have walked this road.

My childhood was spent in a neighborhood where I considered my neighbors as an extension of my family. I was raised Catholic as so many of my neighbors were. Once a week all of us Catholic kids would pile into a car, and a parent would drive us to the other side of town to attend Catechism. There, the teachers taught us stories from the Bible, but seemed to leave out how God's character related to each story. This left me with a lot of unanswered questions about Him. Unfortunately, I was shy and would not ask for the answers to those questions, and I formed the opinion that God was unkind and unloving.

At a Christian outreach and concert, my parents, along with my sister and brother, accepted Christ. I was in elementary school at the time, in one of the lower grades, when they went forward. A woman came and asked me during the altar call if I wanted to go forward. I remember desiring to go, but feeling too shy to say yes, so I told her no.

I attended public school until my last two years of high school. Then I switched to a Christian school. This was an answer to my parents' prayer, which they had placed into the Wailing Wall in Jerusalem, Israel.

I wasn't walking with the Lord. I disliked attending church, but had to in order to stay at the Christian school. My dad reminded me of this fact from time to time, with the words, "When you are eighteen, you can make up your own mind."

Eighteen finally came, so I stopped going to church, and

continued running from the Lord. I wasn't ready to live a life that had no fun in it to follow a bunch of rules. That was what I understood following God to be.

Twenty was the age that I met Dave, who was raised in an unchurched family. Six years after we were married, we found out that we were expecting our first child. This is when my heart started softening toward the Lord.

Shortly after the birth of our daughter, I asked Dave to attend a church with me. I started attending a weekly women's Bible study at this church. One day after a Bible study, I went home, got down on my knees, and asked Jesus into my heart. My running ended that day in the fall of 1991.

As a new believer, I wanted my daughter to hear about the Lord and come to know and accept Him. Alyssa and I prayed at night along with reading stories from her Children's Bible. Alyssa was led to the Lord by her first grade Christian schoolteacher on April 22,1998. She was six years old. Dave accepted the Lord in March of 1998.

In August of 1993, we found out that we were expecting our second child. The pregnancy progressed without any complications, and I was asked to visit my doctor one week after the due date. They hooked me up to a machine, which simulated contractions, so that the doctor could observe our baby's reaction to them. Because of her fright of the loud thumping noise coming out of the machine, Alyssa sat on my mom's lap as the baby kicked. Our baby's kicking was constant throughout most of the test, but suddenly stopped. My doctor returned to the room, and performed an ultrasound. I remember feeling uneasy as I watched my doctor look back and forth from the machine to Alyssa. He did this quite a few times. My doctor told me that the fluid around the baby looked good. He told me to come back after the weekend, and possibly be induced.

I went on Monday to the appointment with my husband and my mom. I was hooked up to the monitor again, but this time the nurse couldn't locate our baby's heartbeat. She left the room, and returned with our doctor. He performed an ultrasound, which confirmed my fear. Our baby had died. Then he sent us to the hospital where he would try to induce labor as my mom called family and friends to pray.

Fifteen hours later, our precious son, Cole, was born. We said hello and goodbye to him all on the same day. We left the hospital with our empty baby seat strapped into the back seat of our car.

Life was unbearable after that. I sank into a deep, dark pit of despair. Everyday I pushed myself to take care of our daughter. There were times when she took care of me.

Alyssa was four days shy of turning three when Cole was born. Needless to say, she didn't quite understand when I told her that he had died.

Twenty-one painful months passed until we found out we were expecting a child. I experienced complications six and a half weeks into the pregnancy. My doctor told me that it was a high-risk pregnancy because blood work and an ultrasound showed the loss of a twin. My body wouldn't cooperate, and attempted to abort our baby on many occasions.

At thirty plus weeks into the pregnancy, once again, my body wouldn't cooperate and I was admitted into the hospital. Five weeks went by. I was confined in bed. My body was working against me with constant contractions and many scares.

Adam was born with an emergency cesarean section on October 9,1996. He was six weeks early, yet very healthy.

A friend gave me this verse from Jeremiah 31:13 (NIV) a day or so before Adam's birth. *"Then maidens will dance and be glad, young men and old as well. I will turn their mourning into gladness; I will give them comfort and joy instead of sorrow."* This same verse was given to me a couple of weeks after losing Cole by a friend of my mother's.

I have learned a lot from these trials, including knowing that all children given to us are gifts from God. We don't have ownership over them, He does. Our job is to love, and raise them with Christian values. We are to continually direct our children to God.

By the way, Adam accepted Jesus on April 30, 2003 at six years of age. Thank you, Jesus!

AUTHOR BIO

Cindy Pocapalia lives in Auburn, California with her husband Dave and their children, Alyssa and Adam. She has been active in children's ministries and co-leading women's Bible studies. Cindy enjoys bike riding, swimming, hiking, and spending time outdoors. She likes having fun with family and friends.

I COME TO THE WATERS

Kathy Ptaszek

I am drawn to water and have been all my life. I come by it naturally; I was raised on the northern Michigan shores of Lake Superior. The cold, clear water of Lake Superior forever spoiled me, it set the standard by which all other water is measured.

Once, I swam in a body of water called Pleasant Lake; it gave new meaning to the term, *misnomer*. It was water, it was wet, and it was a lake, but it was anything but pleasant. Wading into the murky water, I cringed as mud squished through my toes and weeds wrapped around my ankles. I always felt clean and refreshed after a swim in Lake Superior. Climbing out of Pleasant Lake, I felt the need to shower.

We took a boat ride later that day, and encountered the aquatic version of rush hour. We maneuvered around fishermen casting lines from their motorboats. We avoided flags bobbing above brave souls who were attempting to scuba dive. (I figured it was a toss-up between being brave and fool-hearty to search out what bottom-dwellers lurked in such waters.) Powerboats cut a swath through it all, sending up a wall of spray as they whizzed by, water-skiers in tow. I was a nervous wreck by the time we pulled in to shore.

My expectations for that day gave one last *glub* before disappearing into the murky depths of Pleasant Lake. I felt sorry for people who had never experienced Lake Superior; they truly believed this was the good life! They didn't know what they were missing.

My life before Christ was figuratively one big swim in Pleasant Lake; one by one, my hopes and dreams sank to the bottom. I recklessly cannon-balled into those muddy waters in my college years when I began looking to alcohol, drugs, and relationships for pain relief. I found that those waters were shark-infested. They were choked with weeds, whose tentacles pulled me under repeatedly. Date rape, expulsion from college, and an unplanned pregnancy were just some of the consequences of my substance abuse. It all fell so short of what it had promised.

At the ripe age of nineteen, I resigned myself to the fact that I was unlovable. My heart was forming scar tissue as a result of my involvement in unhealthy relationships. I signed on with the budding feminist's movement of the late '60's to formally declare my indifference to men. Pretending I didn't care eased the gut-wrenching ache of loneliness I felt inside.

I was surprised and overjoyed to find true love in my twentieth year. Jon and I were married six months later. Our love was greater than anything I had ever dared to dream. We would have never hurt each other intentionally, but time and again, our alcohol and drug abuse inflicted painful wounds. We were out of control, and our marriage was in danger of going under.

Just in time, my sister tossed me the life-ring of the gospel of Jesus Christ. I desperately clutched it as only a drowning person can. She used my fascination with the occult and psychic divination to interest me in *The Late Great Planet Earth*, a book on Bible prophecy. I was amazed to read of the prophecies regarding Christ's first coming, His death, resurrection, and His soon return. My eyes were opened to the reality of Jesus Christ and my need for a Savior.

Morally, emotionally, and spiritually bankrupt from six years of treading the swamp waters of my alcoholism, I came ashore, sin-stained and in need of divine cleansing. I found this verse, "'*Come now, let us reason together,' says the Lord. 'Though your sins are like scarlet, they shall be as white as snow; though they are as red as crimson, they shall be like wool.'*" (Isaiah 1:18, NIV)

In 1972, I walked in to a Good Friday service, found a seat, and prayed, "Lord, I know I am a sinner, and I believe Christ died for me. Forgive me my sins, in Jesus' name, Amen." The music and message of that day spoke tenderly and personally to me as I began this new relationship with God. When I walked out of that church and into the sunshine of that brisk, spring day, I knew I had been cleansed both inside and out. Like a leper healed of her scourge, I wanted to shout, "I'm clean! I'm clean!"

God not only delivered me from my alcoholism, but the Holy Spirit did a major housecleaning on the inside. I stopped being the angry scorekeeper in our marriage and took my place alongside my husband, giving him his rightful place as head of our household. Eight months later Jon received Christ as his Savior. It was as if we fell in love all over again as we were now united in our faith.

We became active in a Bible-teaching church where we were able to grow and serve as youth workers. We chose as our life verse, Psalm 34:3, *"Glorify the Lord with me; let us exalt His name together."* We loved and served the Lord together for nineteen years until Jon died from leukemia in 1991. God's grace has been sufficient through it all.

In the years that I abused alcohol, no amount ever satisfied my thirst. *"Jesus said, 'Everyone who drinks this water will be thirsty again, but whoever drinks the water I give him will never thirst. Indeed, the water I give him will become in him a spring of water welling up to eternal life.'"*(John 4:13-14, NIV). Like the woman at the well, I responded with, *"...Sir, give me this water so that I won't get thirsty and have to keep coming here to draw water."* (John 4:15, NIV).

I have compassion for those who tread the murky waters of their own "Pleasant Lake," whether it contains alcohol, drugs, pornography, or wealth. They drink that swamp water, and think, "This is the good life!" They don't know what they're missing. Jesus offers this invitation, *"...Whoever is thirsty, let him come; and whoever wishes, let him take the free gift of the water of life."* (Rev. 22:17b, NIV)

I am at a loss to describe how that first drop of Living Water both completely satisfied my thirst and also created a longing for more. This much I know: I am drawn to this Water; it is the standard that all other water is measured by. I refuse to settle for anything less.

AUTHOR BIO

Kathy Ptaszek is a Licensed Social Worker and Certified Addiction Counselor in Hancock, Michigan. She has two grown daughters, Aimee and Molly. Through her writing and speaking ministry, Kathy's desire is to exalt Jesus' name and encourage women to a closer walk with God.

CONSIDER THE LILLIES

Kathy Ptaszek

The checkbook sat unopened. The reality was hitting home: there just was not enough money. The stack of bills on the table required ten times the amount of money in my account. With two children in college and my daughter's wedding nearing, the monthly budget was just the tip of my financial iceberg. In September of 1998, agency cutbacks reduced my workweek to three days, and my paycheck had shrunk proportionately. I had managed to tread water for a while, but after six months, I was about to go under.

I wasn't a rookie at stretching a budget. When our first daughter, Aimee, was born in 1977, my husband, Jon and I agreed that I would quit my job. Since then I had refined penny pinching down to an art form. I planned menus from the weekly supermarket sales. I clipped manufacturer's coupons and saved even more money on our grocery bill. My daughters dressed in brand named clothes that I purchased at garage sales for a fraction of the original cost. Jon marveled more than once, "You sure know how to stretch a dollar."

In spite of my budget-stretching expertise, it was still hard. At times we delayed purchasing necessities. Unexpected car repairs or medical expenses wreaked havoc on our cash flow. Frequently there were shut-off notices on our utilities; I negotiated monthly with the gas company to prevent disconnection. When the books were closed on our family's finances each month, the bottom line was always this: God was faithful.

As new believers in 1972, Jon and I made a decision to tithe our income based on God's promise in Malachi 3:10 (NIV), *"Bring the whole tithe into the storehouse, that there may be food in my house. Test Me in this', says the Lord Almighty, 'and see if I will not throw open the floodgates of heaven and pour out so much blessing that you will not have enough room for it.'"* Since those early years in our marriage, God held true to His promise.

Once we started a family and began living on one income, we discovered that it was harder to keep our tithe commitment. Many times I saw Jon at the kitchen table, the bills piled before him. He would write the check for our tithe first, and then say, "There, I've done my part. I'll pay what bills I can, and the rest is up to God. It's His reputation that is at stake." After my husband's death in 1991, I took over the family finances. I followed Jon's example and paid the tithe first. Until now, February 1999, there had always been enough.

Beyond the bills, I needed a new winter coat, boots, and a dress for Aimee's wedding. The sale catalog sat next to the phone; if I placed the order, that bill would come due in the next thirty days. As I stared at the checkbook, I tried to rationalize that God would understand if I didn't pay my tithe just this once. Finally, I prayed, "Lord, Help me to trust in You. Grant me the faith to believe that You will supply my needs." I picked up the pen, drew a deep breath, and wrote out my tithe.

I spent the next three hours juggling numbers; I stretched the budget until it was about to snap. Exasperated, I put the bills away, and went to bed feeling exhausted and alone. My eyes popped open at 4:00 a.m.; immediately my mind replayed the worries of the previous day. After forty-five minutes of trying to reason with my fears, I admitted defeat. I threw back the covers and made my way downstairs to talk to God.

Opening my Bible, I turned to Matthew 6:25a (NIV) and read, *"Therefore I tell you, do not worry about your life, what you will eat or drink; or about your body, what you will wear."* These were the very things I had on my mind. As I continued to read, God assured me He knew my needs in verses 28-33, *"And why do you worry about clothes? See how the lilies of the field grow. They do not labor or spin. Yet I tell you that not even Solomon in all his splendor was dressed as one of these. If that is how God clothes the grass of the field, which is here today and tomorrow is thrown into the fire, will He not much more clothe you, O you of little faith? So do not worry, saying, 'What shall we eat?' or 'What shall we* drink?' or 'What shall we wear?' For the pagans run after these things, and your heavenly Father knows you need them. But seek first His kingdom and His righteousness, and all these things will be given to you as well."

My prayer was, "Lord, It's me again, Little Faith. I need to feel Your presence. I want to panic. I feel an urgency to do *something*, but I don't know what. I'm afraid to spend any money. You know my need; I'm trusting You to provide." My fears were quieted. I was able to go back to bed, and sleep peacefully until morning.

Two days later, my accountant called to inform me that I was getting a tax refund of $2,700. The new tax credit for parents of college students had resulted in a much larger refund than I anticipated. I paid my bills and bought the clothes I needed.

Later that week, my friend, Marilyn, returned from a vacation in Mexico with a souvenir for me: a hand-painted plate with lilies on it. I was excited to share with her the lesson of the lilies that God had shown me just days before. We marveled that God had prompted her to choose that particular gift; it added such a personal touch to His provision for me. My plate now hangs on the kitchen wall and serves to remind me of God's faithfulness. When circumstances cause my faith to waiver, I need only to consider the lilies.

— AUTHOR BIO —

Kathy Ptaszek is a Licensed Social Worker and Certified Addiction Counselor in Hancock, Michigan. She has two grown daughters, Aimee and Molly. Through her writing and speaking ministry, Kathy's desire is to exalt Jesus' name and encourage women to a closer walk with God.

BECAUSE FOREVER IS A LONG TIME

Chris Quinn

I was raised in a Christian home. My mother was devout, and
practically a Bible-thumper, minus the thumping. My father, though
not a saintly man, was the music minister for a church. So it came as
a bit of a shock to them when, in my pubescent years, I became an
atheist. It was my time to rebel, and I hit them where it hurt.

After a few years, I had matured enough to realize the error of
denouncing beliefs simply because they were those of my parents.
Soon I was a junior in high school, with enough learning under my
belt to understand more complex matters of faith than "Is there
a God?" For most of that first semester, I spent a good deal of time
analyzing wherein I should and should not invest my values.
I graduated into agnosticism, waiting for something that would
give me cause to change.

A funny thing about cancer is that it sure knows how to catch
you off guard. The second half of my junior year was effectively
annulled by the disease. Then, the first semester of my senior year
followed suit. During those months, it seemed I was stuck in an
endless loop of injections, examinations, physical decay, and pain.
My circumstances gave me plenty of time, and reason, for
personal reflection.

I concluded that my choices were fairly clear. Belief in God would
provide me comfort and courage in times of tribulation and suffering.
It would allow me the chance to view the world from a perspective of
love, rather than worldly individualism. And most importantly, I'd
have something to look forward to after my mortal husk had withered
and died.

Inversely, my previous anti-religions would afford me little more
than despair if the world grew too large for me to handle. I would
continue my pitiful existence, wracked with the pain of isolation,

disconnected from my fellow man through my inability to trust. And in the end, I would simple cease to exist.

Even now I shudder at that phrase—cease to exist. It's a scary thought—to be unable to think, to feel, to see, or hear. Lacking the consciousness to know that I had ever been a living, breathing entity.

Concepts such as these would invade my mind at inopportune moments, and I couldn't help but wonder why it had been so hard to simply say, "Yes, I believe." That is all He asked for. It is not a difficult task, nor does it come with a price tag. He asked me to love others and love Him above all.

After a long period of debate, lasting well into my first years in college, I discovered my problem. I had been asking myself the wrong question. Instead of asking why I should believe, I should have been asking "Why not?"

I am now in my final year of college. Soon, I'll be diving headfirst into the real world and trying to make it on my own. But my faith grows stronger with each obstacle I overcome. I may not be a perfect Christian. I still make mistakes, still make bad decisions, and still act completely stupid at times. Somehow, having God in my life makes those problems seem less intimidating. I have made the full rounds and have seen both points of view. And even if I can't prove His existence, I no longer live in fear of my own.

Because forever is a long time to simply *not be*.

— AUTHOR BIO —

Chris Quinn is a freelance artist and graphic designer in Georgia. Besides writing stories and poetry, he is currently studying mass communications and graphic design at Piedmont College. Chris is also an editorial cartoonist and hopes to have his cartoons syndicated in the near future.

SHOWERS AND FLOWERS

Pamela Randles

"April showers bring May flowers"—my favorite time of the year. Spring is in the air; hope is in the air. It's as if April showers wash away the winter and everything dead lives again.

With the coming of spring came a tugging at my heart. A feeling that something was going to happen that would change our lives forever. Being the optimist that I am, I was sure it would be something good. My life is in order. I have a wonderful husband and two beautiful children. And it's spring, the season for living. But as April walked into May in 1998, heaviness wrapped itself around my heart and I wondered.

It was a day like any other. I was headed to the kitchen for my first cup of coffee, when the phone rang. I was surprised to find that the voice at the other end belonged to my husband's boss. "There's been an accident," were the first words out of his mouth. The day that began like any other, would be the day that changed our lives forever.

I called my best friend, who lived next door, and asked her to please come and help get my kids dressed, forgetting for the moment that my children were fourteen and eighteen years old. Myrna sat on the couch watching the confusion. We couldn't figure out how to get dressed. With Myrna's help, we figured it out and managed to get to the hospital.

The days that followed were some of the darkest of my life. We had walked into someone else's nightmare. This couldn't be happening to us.

My husband had been run over by a front-end-loader. His chest was crushed. He was bleeding from the soft tissue so they couldn't stop it. They had to remove his spleen, repair his colon and numerous other things, which I don't care to remember. He was on a ventilator so he couldn't talk, although he was fully conscience for the first two days and nights. It didn't look good. And as one day became another and another, we began to lose hope.

By Friday night, I was so tired I didn't think I could go on. I couldn't eat or sleep. I sat curled up on a small couch in the ICU with my family, somewhere between life and death. Moments earlier the doctor had informed me that my husband probably would not live through the night. I remember walking up that long hallway, wondering how a mother tells her children their daddy isn't going to live through the night.

I sat on my little couch, numb with pain, listening to the sobs of my children. I watched as tears streamed down the faces of those closest to me.

My son, who is usually very affectionate, didn't want to be touched. In all his fourteen years there was nothing I couldn't help him with. I could always make him feel better. But on this night, I couldn't help him. I sat there watching my six foot, two inch son sobbing all alone in the corner with a broken heart, my heart breaking with every sob.

My eighteen-year-old daughter, who is usually very strong and not very cuddly, threw herself into my arms and cried her heart out. Her wonderful daddy, my beautiful husband would never come home again.

All alone in the quiet hallway I sat in a small chair outside my husband's room. The minutes ticked by so slowly that I was sure this night would last forever. The man who lay in that hospital bed barely resembled the man I knew and loved.

They had him mostly uncovered. I could see the damage to his body and he was so badly swollen; I couldn't bear to look. I would squat down by the side of the bed and hold on to the rail. This way I could only see his good shoulder and the side of his face.

When I could stand no longer, I would sit just outside his room until I could get enough strength and courage to go back in.

As I sat there shaking from the inside out, the words of an old song came to mind. In my heart I began to sing. "I'm so glad I learned to trust Him. Just to take Him at His word, and to know that thou art with me, will be with me to the end." That isn't how it goes but that's how it came to me. "Jesus, Jesus, how I trust Him! How I've proved him o'er and o'er! Jesus, Jesus, precious Jesus!" I couldn't remember the words, so I just hummed that last line.

Later that night I was telling my pastor what the doctor had said. He looked at me and said, "It makes me think of the song, *I'm so glad I learned to trust Him.*"

"That's the song!" I said. "But what's the last line?"

"Oh for grace to trust Him more."

It's been five and a half years since I receive the 'grace to trust Him more.' There is one thing I know for sure. Faith is not a feeling. When it feels like God has turned His back and walked away, He hasn't. When I think God isn't there, He is. When I think my life is over, God still has a plan. God can redeem anything. We just need to trust.

--- AUTHOR BIO ---

Pamela Randles resides in a small town near Salem, Oregon. She and her late husband spent many years in ministry and raised two children together, Ellisa and Jason. Pam enjoys writing, singing, and spending time with her family.

GOD'S PRECIOUS CARE

Cheri Roberts

I kissed my four children as they left for school in the fall of 1982. As I watched them innocently walk away, I began to cry. No one knew, not even my husband, that our refrigerator was totally empty, and I didn't know where we would get our next meal.

We lived in a cute, little, white house with black shutters, one block from the Mississippi River in Comanche, Iowa. Our family of six included three sons, one daughter, two dogs, and one cat. We were a faith-filled family, and the Lord had truly blessed us, but He had never allowed us to go without food before in our lives.

The town we lived in was very small, with a population of six thousand people. Since 1980, we had watched as factory after factory either closed down or announced sizeable lay-offs. We heard that there would soon be a lay-off where my husband worked. So in preparation, we had put in a wood stove since we could get all kinds of wood from fallen trees around us. We also put in a sand point well with fresh artesian water so we wouldn't be paying a public water bill. We had canned over one thousand quarts of vegetables, tomato juice, pickles, and sauerkraut. I froze banana and zucchini breads. We bought several hundred pounds of potatoes and onions stored in a bin in the basement, all in hopes of self-sufficiency. Or so we thought!

When we got the notice of his lay-off, we were not really alarmed because we had been through this twice before. But this time was different. This time we were told it was permanent. For a man who had been working all of his life since the age of thirteen, not to have work at the age of forty-two was devastating.

He applied everywhere. He was willing to work anywhere just to have a job. He finally was hired as a contract mail carrier, driving a truck three hours a day. It was forty-five miles from home in the quad cities, but praise God, it was a job!

With that distance, and the price of gas, we couldn't afford for him to come home every night. If he had stayed in a hotel, we wouldn't have made any money, so he decided that he would sleep in his pick-up truck at night. Then he'd come home on the week-ends.

While he was at home, I would do his laundry and get another big lunch packed, while he spent time playing with the children.

As winter came, it was very cold, sometimes down to thirty degrees below zero. He took a heavy sleeping bag. I knitted him slippers, a stocking cap and a scarf. As he drove off, I hoped that we had thought of everything to help him stay warm.

He was concerned about how we could keep this up, as our supplies were now depleted, and we were notified that our medical insurance would run out. With all of this in the back of his mind, I couldn't bring myself to tell him that the canned goods were gone, and I had sent the last of the groceries with him.

As the children left for school that day, I can remember standing in the kitchen praying through tears, asking the Lord what I was going to do! Now I was starting to understand why there are prostitutes and bank robbers. I knew the Lord had blessed me with these children, and said, "Surely You don't want me to watch them go hungry!" Then in my thoughts I heard, "Read My Word, my child!"

Now I was scared, worried and in doubt, and responded, "I'm sure that will take care of it! How will that feed my family?" And softly He repeated, "Read My Word."

In desperation I went to our bedroom, threw myself on the floor next to my bed and opened the Bible. The passage that opened was Matthew 6:25-27 (NIV), *"Therefore I tell you, do not worry about your life, what you eat or drink; or about your body, what you will wear. Is not life more important than food, and the body more important than clothes? Look at the birds of the air; they do not sow or reap or store away in barns, and yet your heavenly Father feeds them. Are you not much more valuable than they? Who of you by worrying can add a single hour to his life?"*

I stood up with a faith that I had never known before. It welled up inside of me. "Okay, Lord, in your Word You have just said that You care so much for us, even more than the birds, so I'm going to believe You know our need, and somehow You will feed my family tonight! And we normally eat at 5:30 pm!"

That day was filled with the usual cleaning, laundry, and dishes. All the while doubts and questions came. *How is God going to do this?* Then I went back and reread the same Scripture to strengthen my faith. Another thought filtered through my mind. *Tell someone. How else can this happen?* As I reread the Scripture over and over again, I reminded myself what the Lord had said to me. It was apparent that the birds did not tell anyone of their need! God just fed them. So that was what I was going to believe! It was clear that the One who needed to know, already knew my predicament. As doubts crept in, I read and reread the Scripture out loud all day.

Soon the children were home asking what we were going to have to eat. I just looked at them and answered that I wasn't quite sure.

At 4:30 pm, there was a knock at the door. As I opened it, there stood a high school friend. She said that she had heard we were still not working full time. She had a box in her hands and asked if we would mind eating her meal from the day before. She said they were leaving town for a game and were fearful it wouldn't keep until they got back. To my amazement I could see ham, scalloped potatoes, green beans and even a pie. I assured her that she was not offending me, and then shared with her what I had prayed all day!

With tears of joy in our eyes, I thanked her, we hugged and she left for the game. Praising and thanking God for this wonderful blessing, I went into the kitchen to warm the food. We sat down, shared grace and I looked up. It was 5:30 pm!

The story does not end here. This was the beginning of a two-year multiplication of food, clothing, and the love of God to and through our home and out to many other people. Our God cares about every need of His children.

──────── AUTHOR BIO ────────
Cheri Roberts is married to Dennis. They have
four children—Mark, Todd, Brent and Tayla. As a six-
year-old, she was inspired by her maternal grandmother
to pray. At age thirty-two, she began a deeper and
more exciting relationship with Jesus that truly brought
power and blessings through prayer.

IDENTITY CRISIS

Jennifer A. Roberts

I have been saved for nearly eighteen years, but it wasn't until my identity crisis that I began to experience my identity in Christ.

Earlier this year, I was attending a celebration for my stepfather who was appointed superintendent of a school district in Texas. I was standing in the receiving line as countless community officials, teachers, administrators, public servants, and students congratulated him on his new position. My stepsister, who had just graduated from nursing school only days earlier, was standing to my left, and I listened as people were also congratulating her on her achievement. Many asked what she was going to do next and she cheerfully indulged each one as I stood by, smiling politely, awaiting the dreaded question, "And what do you do?"

This question always sends chills up my spine because my answer is rarely sufficient, and it usually prompts people to offer advice on how I could be doing something else. As I told each person that I was a homemaker, most of them said, "Oh, that's nice," or gave me a smile that gave the same sentiment, but none of them were impressed or intrigued.

Out of all the people in the receiving line, there were two well-wishers who stood out the most. Like many others before them, the couple asked me what I did for a living, but when I told them that I was a homemaker, the husband gave me a look of disappointment. He proceeded to say, "No! I thought for sure you'd say that you were a career woman, an executive…" His wife quickly chimed in and added, "or a model."

My heart immediately sank as they continued to look at me as though I were in a casket. They literally seemed to mourn for me. And what's worse, I mourned for myself because I didn't have a career of which I was proud. But as much as I hurt on the inside, I managed to keep a smile plastered across my face.

Their comments cut deeply for two reasons. The first was because I knew that I could be all of the things that he and his wife had named. In fact, I *had* been a career woman until God pulled me aside and said, "I have other plans for you." It had been excruciatingly painful to trade in my agenda for God's, but I was well on my way. It was speed bumps like this experience that often made it difficult to proceed.

The second reason I was hurt was because of the low value these two people had on my career as a homemaker. My work didn't count for much in their eyes. Their words and looks asked me in no uncertain terms, "Why are you a homemaker when you could be doing so much more with your life?" *Ouch.*

It was at this gathering that I began to see just how synonymous my identity was with my career. The experience made me feel insignificant and exposed because I didn't have a career outside of the house. It was at this point that God began to show me whose I was because my heart was finally open to receive it.

Even though I didn't recognize it, God knew that my source of value, worth, contentment, fulfillment, and approval had been my career and through a painful circumstance He helped me to know that I was His child and that He was enough.

One Monday morning in my personal Bible study, I began to look up verses on worth, value, and work. Initially, I didn't find what I was looking for, but I continued to study until I struck gold. I found exactly what I was looking for in 1 John 3:1 (NIV) which says, *"How great is the love the Father has lavished on us, that we should be called children of God! And that is what we are! The reason the world does no know us is that it did not know him."* I wanted to breathe in the words of God and meditate on them because they were so sweet. They were like a cool breeze on a hot day.

This single verse made me want to leap for joy because it told me that I was fine just the way I am. I am a child of God, and that is enough. God had clearly spoken the words I was waiting to hear, *I want you. I need you to come and be a part of Me. I need you to serve me.* I knew this as head knowledge, but for the first time, I *experienced* this with my heart. God had imparted such wonderful wisdom to me. He said, "You can be fulfilled and discover your purpose in Me." I experienced the acceptance and fullness of God in a new and different way. Even though I loved God, I had been looking for purpose, fulfillment, and acceptance from the world.

I thank God for teaching me the difference between His love and the world's. The world's love is based on my performance; God's love is based on Jesus' performance at Calvary. The world's acceptance of me has everything to do with what I am, what I have, and what I can give; God's love is based on who He is and who I am in Him. My identity was once connected to my position in life. This was a perilous place to be because when I no longer had a position, I no longer had an identity. God taught me that I will have many positions in life as a daughter, sister, wife, mother, possibly even an entrepreneur, but I will only have one identity and that is as His child.

AUTHOR BIO

Jennifer Roberts is a wife and full-time homemaker. She is also the founder of Ladies in Waiting, a ministry that helps women develop a more intimate relationship with Christ. She enjoys writing Christian literature and is an active member of her church's newsletter, and couple's and family life ministries.

THE BRIDE'S VICTORY

Susanne Scheppmann

"Grandpa, I don't know how to die. I just don't get it. How do you die?" she asked. "I am tired of battling all of this."

Motioning for another dose of painkillers, Breana's waxen face relayed frustration. Her blond, pageboy wig sat slightly askew as if to punctuate her question.

With a wrinkled, trembling hand, he patted her wig back into place. His eyes filled with tears as he shrugged his shoulders without an answer. No one in the room volunteered a response to the baffled fifteen-year-old, as her mom, Jayme, administered the needed pain relief.

After a seventeen-month, grueling war with cancer, Breana faced her last battle: death. Although her spirit remained indomitable, her young athletic body could no longer continue fighting. Family, friends, pastors, and medical professionals circled around day after day in support.

Doctors had watched her win decisive victories over chemotherapy and radiation treatments. Respect filled their voices as they conferred with each other and spoke of her tenacity and ability to bounce back. She amazed her family when she triumphed over each surgery and recovered her teen enthusiasm for life. Friends who came to give support found themselves cheered on by Breana in their own life struggles. Pastors turned her story into sermons, illustrating a walk of faith and trust. Though not one of them knew the answer to her question, "How do I die?"

However, God knew the answer to her dilemma. Before the question popped from her lips, the answer was on its way.

The doorbell rang. An acquaintance stood at the doorway and appeared unsure of herself. She said, "I hope this doesn't seem too presumptuous, but I feel God wanted me to bring this book to Breana." She offered, in an extended hand, a sky-blue book. The title,

Heaven Your Real Home, jumped out as Jayme, Breana's mother, reached for it.

"Thank you," Jayme replied politely, uncertain of just what she thought of the gift.

Walking back to Breana, she placed the book into her thin hand. Immediately, Breana began to scan the pages. Intrigued by what she saw, she read a few pages. The author, Joni Eareckson Tada, described the reality and delight of heaven with clarity. She wrote eagerly and expectantly of her own desire of heaven.

With a slurred, medicated voice, Breana said, "Well, even if I don't know how to die, I guess heaven will be more than I can imagine. This book brings me peace, Mom."

However, the book was only a part of God's answer to her question of "How do I die?" Weekly groups met to pray for Breana and her family. One night in prayer, God nudged Laura, a local artist to draw a picture for Breana.

Inspired, she began the charcoal drawing immediately. She drew. She erased. She pondered and prayed. God directed each detail. Laura drew at a frenzied pace. She felt the need to complete the picture quickly. Within days, the work of art sat finished, framed, and ready for delivery.

Meanwhile, each time Breana felt anxiety, she requested the book, which she had renamed her "*Peace Book*." She read it to herself. She read portions to anyone who sat by her bed. Calmness crept into her wan face. Still she wondered, "How do I die?"

The doorbell rang. Once again, a hesitant friend stood holding a gift. Handing over a large wrapped package, she greeted Jayme nervously.

"Hi, Jayme. This is from someone who wants to remain anonymous. We hope it blesses Breana and your family." Fumbling for words she finished with, "We feel this gift was directed by God."

Breana's dark-circled eyes watched expectantly as Jayme undid the wrapping around the package. Gasping, the family stared at the picture. It was a portrait of Breana dressed in a bridal gown, gliding down a path to meet a groom.

She stood tall and straight; the long white bridal dress fell gracefully to her feet. Elegant, yet simple it revealed flawless skin. The skin showed no weaving of surgical scars. It seemed as if a halo of pure health enveloped her.

Her face in the portrait mesmerized everyone. Her countenance reflected the anticipation of bridal joy. Her eyes sparkled. Breana's smile radiated with such completeness that everything else paled in comparison. She was smiling at the groom.

The groom's head was turned toward Breana. Upon his head sat a stately crown. A robe draped down from his broad shoulders with a sash that read, "King of Kings and Lord and Lords."

As they studied the picture, they realized a small rock ledge ran along the path. Upon the ledge lay a small book with its side binding revealing the title, "*Peace Book*." Breana appeared to rush past the book, toward the groom who held out his hand. The bride saw only the groom beckoning for her.

The doorbell chimed, again. This time high school friends trooped in and circled Breana's chair. It was prom night. Dressed in sparkly dresses they crowded around for Jayme to take their pictures together with Breana. Enjoying her friends' excitement and youthful enthusiasm, she pointed to her portrait with a weak grin.

"My dress," she struggled to say.

"It's beautiful!" "Oh, you look gorgeous!"

She nodded wistfully.

As her friends left, Breana pondered the picture. An illusive message seemed to emit from it.

"Oh well, I just don't get it. I'm tired. Mom, I want to go to sleep."

A fitful night ensued. Breana mumbled unintelligible words. Sitting on the edge of the bed, Jayme asked, "Do you want your *Peace Book*?"

Shaking her head, Breana appeared confused and disoriented.

A doorbell tinkled faintly from a distance.

Suddenly, in a clear, healthy voice, Breana said, "I get it! I get it!"

"What is it? What do you get?" her mother asked.

Breana stared wide-eyed into the darkness of the bedroom and said, "He's watching me."

"Is it Jesus, Breana?"

Speechless, she nodded.

Crying, her mother said, "Take his hand, baby. Take his hand."

Jayme lifted the bride's battle worn hand into the air and placed it into the Groom's invisible hand. A sigh of satisfaction escaped from the bride's lips as she started down the path with her Groom to eternal life.

Breana finally had her answer. She knew how to die. She had won the final battle. The bride was victorious.

— AUTHOR BIO —

Susanne Scheppmann is a freelance writer and Christian speaker who resides in Las Vegas, Nevada. In addition, she serves as Women's Ministries Director for her church, The Crossing. Breana was the daughter of a dear friend of Susanne's.

BE PRETTY

Lisa Schroeder

"Nana, make me look pretty!" I sobbed to my grandmother that afternoon many years ago. I had seen my mother trim my bangs dozens of times, and knew I could do it myself. Unfortunately, at just five years old, it didn't occur to me to use a mirror.

After hearing Nana tell the story throughout my childhood, I'm not sure how much I actually remember, and how much just seems like a memory after picturing it in my mind so many times. Looking back now, the memory I recall most strongly is the love and concern Nana's voice held as she told of how she struggled in vain to even out the little hair that was left. I knew each time she told the story, Nana would have given her right arm to make me "look pretty." Papa, my grandfather, was just as fond of me. As the first grandchild, I was perfect in their eyes and experienced not only unconditional love and acceptance, but something even rarer—their attention. I was the apple of their eyes, and they always made time for me.

My parents worked long hours and were always busy once they got home in the evenings. I enjoyed my grandparents' frequent visits, spent time at their house each summer, and even accompanied them on some camping trips. My happiest times were spent when I visited their home alone. Late at night, snuggled up under Nana's handmade quilts in the spare bedroom, I could overhear them discussing me. Each night they talked over concerns and worries, as if I were the most important topic in the world. To them, I was.

Although I knew Nana and Papa intimately, this early memory is the only time I remember my grandmother being concerned with how I looked. Perhaps that was because Nana was not very pretty in the world's eyes. Being very poor, she did without make-up, saved my grandpa's old flannel shirts for her jackets, and sewed all of her own clothes in simple, practical styles. She never had much and always made do.

For someone so unconcerned with looks, surprisingly, Nana's favorite saying was, "Be pretty." I heard it before I went to school, when I received an invitation to a party, and of course when I began to date. Pleasant images of girls in formal attire, drinking tea with pinkies outstretched, came to mind when I heard this frequent admonition. For some reason I never truly grasped the meaning of the words until my teen years, and then it was too late.

It started with comparatively small things such as lying to my parents about whom I was hanging around with, but quickly advanced to sneaking out at night and getting involved in all the things parents fear most. Before I knew what had happened, I ended up pregnant. It was then that I realized the meaning of Nana's warning, "Be pretty," but I couldn't undo the damage I had done. How I suddenly wanted to BE pretty! I no longer cared about make-up, clothes, or anything else. I suddenly longed for the traditional values I had once thought so old fashioned.

At that time, there was still enough shame and embarrassment attached to being an unwed pregnant teenager to make for a miserable nine months. At home, my life was a nightmare. My mother, who was a new Christian, agreed to let me live at home and raise my child, but it came with an emotional price. I was basically in trouble for the duration of the pregnancy. There was no joy or anticipation over this coming addition; there were constant sighs and comments to remind me how difficult I had made my parents' lives. No one cared or asked if it was difficult on me, but the most difficult part was still to come. Outside the house, I avoided my friends, kept busy at my summer job, and discreetly hid the top of my pants as the buttons ceased to fasten. The time was coming when it would be impossible to hide the change in my stomach, and I knew what that meant. In August, my summer job would end and we would leave on our annual vacation. That was the non-negotiable date my parents set for me to break the news to my grandparents. Telling Nana would be difficult enough, but my greatest fear was telling Papa. I didn't know how I could ever utter such a shameful thing to him, or how an eighty-two-year-old man would take it.

My mother was letting our long-distance relatives know, but telling Nana and Papa myself was part of my punishment. How

I longed for a little encouragement from my parents, but all I received were comments such as, "There's no telling what your grandfather will do. He has such a temper," and the constant reminder, "He thinks you can do no wrong. This will crush him."

The night before our trip, we went to my grandparents for dinner. I wasn't showing yet, but my tight, uncomfortable clothes were almost unbearable with the August heat and my overwhelming anxiety. As I somehow made it through dinner, a plan began to slowly form. Papa always walked us out to the car, but Nana avoided the steps after dark. If I waited until everyone else was out of the house, I could tell Nana first, while Papa was outside. Gathering courage, I lingered behind as my parents started for the door.

Ushering Nana into the kitchen, I blurted out, "I have to tell you something." If I live to be a thousand, I'll never understand the mercy that was shed on me that night. This woman, most beautiful of all women to me, with an inside as pretty as they come, melted my heart with these words, "You're pregnant, aren't you?"

I nearly collapsed as I nodded. Holding my shoulders, she looked me in the eyes, and with a love I had never known said "You go ahead on vacation, and I'll tell Papa while you're gone."

Somehow, I hugged her and made it out the door. I don't know what happened during those two weeks. I never had the courage to ask, and Nana never mentioned it again during her life. All I know is that when I returned from vacation, wearing maternity clothes, Nana and Papa treated me with as much love as they ever had.

A few weeks later I began to attend church with my mother. It was there I learned of the One who loves unconditionally, and I found mercy and grace at His feet. By the time Christopher entered our lives that Christmas, both Nana and Papa, and my parents thought the world of him, and I finally felt forgiven.

It wasn't until months later that I discovered Nana had begun to attend church with a friend. Although she had always talked about believing in God, this new relationship with her Savior changed her from the inside out. As near as I have been able to determine, her relationship with the Lord began shortly before that warm August night.

AUTHOR BIO

Lisa Schroeder is married to Hal, and is the mother of Chris, Kaja, and Trina. She lives in southern California and has home-schooled since 1991. Lisa enjoys quilting, embroidery, in-depth Bible study, and tea parties.

God's Helping Hand

David Schuitema

Two friends and I were playing Monopoly in a rural trailer park in Alaska when there was a sudden knock at the door. We opened the door and found the woman from next door frantically asking us to come help her husband who was choking.

Without hesitation, Dale called 911, and Carl and I ran next door. As I came through the door, it was obvious that the man was unconscious in his chair. His head was back, limp, and his face blue. I noticed a partially eaten steak on the man's plate. We knew we had to act fast.

The gentleman was a large man, making it impossible for us to effectively perform the Heimlich maneuver in this situation. Realizing we had to clear the man's airways, we lowered him to the floor. I reached in his mouth with my fingers to check for the obstruction as Carl checked for a heartbeat and then a pulse. There were none.

As I stretched my fingers to their maximum extension, I could just feel the obstruction with the very tip of my finger, but I couldn't manage to get a hold of it. It was at this time that I uttered a prayer from the very depths of my soul. It wasn't fancy or eloquent, merely an audible "God, help me!" Immediately on the utterance of those words, the obstruction moved up into my grasp on its own. I pulled it out and we began CPR on the man immediately.

After a few minutes, which seemed like an eternity, the man took a huge breath and began to snore loudly. It was a beautiful sound.

The paramedics arrived shortly after the man began breathing, his pulse was picking up. Once we had briefed them on what had taken place, I walked on trembling legs back to Dale's house. Shaking and sobbing, I realized I had just experienced a direct encounter with God in my life.

I had never been so terrified as I was that day, staring into the face of death. Nor had I ever been so thankful for God's merciful intervention in this man's life. God still performs miracles today. I've seen it first hand and will never forget that cold Alaska night as long as I live.

─AUTHOR BIO─

David Schuitema lives in Covington, Georgia with his wife Valerie, daughters Alyssa, Megan and son, Davis. David helps with youth and recovery ministries at his church and works as an aircraft maintenance technician at a major airline. He enjoys all aspects of the outdoors, working on projects around the house, reading, playing the banjo, and drawing.

RESURRECTION POWER!

Gwen Shannon

I personally experienced the miraculous touch of Jesus as He so creatively set me free from depression. God's touch in my life was not only evidence of resurrection power, but was a creation of new life. *"Therefore, if anyone is in Christ, he is a new creation; the old has gone, the new has come!"* (II Corinthians 5:17, NIV)

Although I was a believer and regularly attended church, I lived in the darkness of my mind, unable to see the true hope of knowing Jesus. I felt formless and empty. But, as a baptized child of the living God, the Holy Spirit was hovering within. I had not been forgotten. The Holy Spirit was poised, waiting to begin a new creation process within my mind in God's perfect timing.

I sought professional help for the suicidal depression that plagued me through hospitalization, counseling, and medications. In my case, none of the standard treatments proved to be effective. I developed intolerance to the anti-depressant medications with serious side effects and seemed to sink lower and lower as the years passed. But God's healing power is greater and more creative than anything we can imagine. God's move in my life was so amazingly different that it shattered the box in which I had placed Him!

I knew God for salvation, but had no victory in my life. I had received forgiveness for my sins through the blood of Jesus, and I confessed Jesus as my personal Savior, yet I was not able to be a radiant witness of Jesus to anyone else! The sin and oppression that haunted me prevented me from fulfilling God's call for my life.

Then one day, God burst out of the box of limitations in which I had kept Him by beginning a most unique process of healing. As I was driving home from the bank, I had a Christian tape playing in the car. Although the volume was fairly loud, it seemed to fade as I began to hear another song in my ear. The song I heard was a full performance as if on the radio. There was a band and a singer. The song seemed to be called "Cry of Anguish" and had three verses with an unforgettable refrain that continued to repeat in my mind.

When I arrived at my house, I felt compelled to play the melody on the piano and write the words. As soon as I wrote the words, the song in my inner hearing stopped! As I re-read the words, a story of God's great love emerged as a soothing balm for a soul in anguish. Needless to say, I was amazed and perplexed as I recited the lyrics of the song that day.

At this particular time in my life, I was unaware that the Holy Spirit indeed brings songs to people in this miraculous way. But soon I discovered the Scripture that explains this phenomenon. In Psalm 32:7 (NIV) David said: *"You are my hiding place; you will protect me from trouble and surround me with songs of deliverance."* My loving Savior, Jesus Christ, was surrounding me with sweet songs of deliverance, preparing my heart for complete healing by whispering words of hope in my ears.

I continued to hear a new song in full performance daily for thirty days. Although the styles of music varied from loud, upbeat praise choruses to soft hymns, the message was the same. The lyrics all proclaimed God's healing power and offered reassurance of His love. Each song would continue repeatedly in my ear, until I played the melody on the piano and wrote the words. After the supernatural experience of the first song, I noticed that I had a new desire to live to the next day. My desire upon awakening was to hear another song! My will to live was returning as the love of God was saturating my soul.

Finally, I became brave enough to tell a few friends about this occurrence, and they gathered around me to pray. They understood that God had begun this creative experience to heal me and prayed for complete healing and deliverance from the depression that had held me captive for years.

God was merciful and did indeed completely heal me after that prayer. I knew a peace in my soul and stability in my mind as never before. It was a miraculous display of God's resurrection power in my life.

It was not a coincidence that my pastor was preaching a series on God's grace during this time. I was now able to grasp the true meaning of grace, and I believe that this new understanding helped to secure the healing that God gave me. I continued to hear songs for several months after that amazing healing prayer. The new, joyous tunes proclaimed victory and resurrection life in Christ.

I still write songs for the Lord and offer my life in service to Him by leading a prayer group. God has revealed to me the power of prayer and strengthened my faith so I no longer limit Him with my own expectations. It is the desire of my life to grow closer to Jesus with a completely surrendered heart *"...that I may know Him and the power of His resurrection..."* (Philippians 3:10, NKJV)

AUTHOR BIO

Gwen Shannon of League City, Texas is a wife, mother, teacher, and founder of the women's praise and prayer ministry called "Women Take Action," uniting Houston's Bay Area in prayer.

THANKFUL HEART

Candace Sorondo

While I do not care for the changes in my forty-eight-year-old body, I do appreciate the vantage-point I enjoy as I look back over the years. The Lord has spent my entire life teaching me that it is in the darkest days that the most important lessons are learned. It is in those bleak seasons that my dependence on Him leads me to a special place, a place that eludes me during my good times. It is a place of comfort and oneness with the Lord. When stability in my life begins to crumble and things are turned up side down, I hang on to Jesus. My life whirls around me as a tornado, but at the center of the storm, Jesus sits with me. It is then that I am ready to learn.

One turbulent season in my life occurred about eighteen years ago. It seemed that everywhere I looked in my life things were breaking down. In the span of one year, my grandfather descended into Alzheimer's disease, my folks split up after years of alcoholism and mental abuse. My sister's husband left his family, rendering the rest of us heartbroken. My own husband was not earning an income as he completed an internship required for entrance into his chosen profession.

I supported our little family (we had a one-year-old son) by waiting tables. My husband could not handle not supporting his family, and I couldn't handle everything else that had taken place. Things seemed to spiral down, and at the lowest point, it looked like my husband and I would not make it. We were headed for breakup.

Late one summer night, after working a late shift and then drowning some of my pain in alcohol, I sat outside under a beautiful sky. I was completely miserable and at the end of myself. I looked up to the heavens and asked, "God, are You up there? I've made such a terrible mess of everything. If You are there, take over my life because I just can't do it." Right there I surrendered my life to the Lord. And that is where the turn started.

My folks never reunited and my sister's husband never came back, but I was able to give up feeling that I was helpless. My husband and I recommitted to each other, and when my husband began again to earn a salary, his heaviest burden lifted. We received some counseling and dug in to do the work of making a happy marriage.

Months went by and our life turned around. Shortly after, I learned I was pregnant. My daughter was born a month early on Thanksgiving Day. We knew she was a gift from the Lord and that He was affirming to us that in the midst of any circumstance, there is reason to rejoice and keep a grateful heart. In the years that followed, there were happy seasons and some sad ones too. I have learned to embrace Ecclesiastes 3:1-15 (NIV). *"There is a time for everything, and a season for every activity under heaven..."* And when the road gets rough I need only to look at my daughter for the reminder to rejoice in all things.

────────── AUTHOR BIO ──────────

Candace Soronda is a wife and mother of two teenagers. She works as a waitress and is very active in the small charismatic church she attends where she helps lead the worship dance team.

TIFFANY'S FAITH

Charles Stone

After I squirted a glob of gooey, caramel colored, antibiotic soap on my hands, to my dismay, I couldn't find a faucet on my sink. At a loss to wash my hands, I glanced to my left and noticed that when the surgeon leaned against his sink, water flowed out of the goose necked spigot. When I mimicked him, water gently flowed out in a gentle stream without getting my blue scrubs wet. I then worked up a lather with the bristly, sterilized sponge and focused on my fingernails as the nurse had instructed.

As I scrubbed, my thoughts drifted to a nameless father who stood in the exact same place perhaps two hours earlier as had hundreds of dads before him. A new lease on life, permanent disability, or even death awaited that dad's child. The same possibilities awaited my daughter. My fears would soon turn to faith through the unintended instruction of my five-year-old daughter.

Five years earlier, joy overwhelmed me as I nestled my newborn, Tiffany, in my arms for the first time. We experienced a problem-free first year with Tiffany, every parent's dream. That dream came to an abrupt end that fateful Christmas day one year later. Unbeknownst to us, Tiffany would soon become our greatest teacher of authentic faith.

That year we spent Christmas with my wife, Sherryl's, parents in the small town of Laurel, Mississippi. Christmas morning arrived with the expected commotion that three excited preschoolers bring. Sherryl's dad strategically placed the video camera to capture our three kids' delighted expressions as they skipped into the living room to see the mound of gifts stacked beneath the tree. After we thanked Jesus for his gifts to us, we excitedly watched as they tore into the colorfully wrapped packages. After what seemed like forever, they opened the last gift, and we moved into the kitchen for our Christmas breakfast.

As the two older kids sat at the table, I took highchair duty with Tiffany. I cajoled Tiffany to eat her pureed peaches and scrambled eggs, and I noticed something unusual about her right eye. It seemed to quiver. It frightened us because none of our other kids did this. The next day, a pediatrician saw Tiffany and told us not to worry about this common condition. But he did suggest that we see a pediatric eye specialist. Upon our return home to Atlanta we immediately saw the specialist. After his examination, he too encouraged us not to worry, but scheduled a CT scan just to be sure. The doctor promised to call should anything unusual show up on the scan.

A few days later as we returned from the scan, the phone rang. I answered the phone, and the words I would soon hear would forever change our lives. The doctor tried to minimize the weight of the message as much as he could. He first said that the scan showed an irregularity, a lesion. I thought to myself, *A lesion . . . could that be something simple that antibiotics could treat?* When he could no longer delay the inevitable, the words he spoke next felt like a kick in the stomach. He stoically said, "Your daughter has a brain tumor."

I don't remember how I ended the conversation, nor do I remember how I broke the news to my wife. I do remember that my mind began to spin as I wept uncontrollably and held our tiny daughter in my arms. Life would now take on new meaning, as we would fight to save her life.

Four years after that fateful day and after two brain surgeries, multiple doctors' visits, and years of therapy, another dangerous brain surgery now confronted Tiffany. However, even through her three years of pain, she exuded a faith that far exceeded her years. In a poignant way, her faith would soon lift ours.

In the months prior, she had learned her alphabet by memorizing Scripture verses. A Bible verse corresponded to each letter of the alphabet. She learned the verse, *". . .all have sinned and fall short of the glory of God"* (Romans 3:23, NIV) for the letter A, *". . .believe in the Lord Jesus, and you will be saved. . ."* (Acts 16:31, NIV), for the letter B and so on. Before we left for the hospital, I asked Tiffany what verse she would choose as a theme verse for the upcoming surgery. She made her selection and planted the verse in her heart. This verse would soon stir us to a new level of faith.

After I scrubbed for five minutes, I rinsed the soapy, yellow foam off my hands and dried them. As the nurse tied the white, paper mask around my mouth, she said the surgeons were now ready. I walked into the narrow hallway, where Tiffany sat in her kid-sized wheelchair and slowly wheeled her into the cold, bright operating room. The anesthesiologist pointed to the small metal operating table and asked me to lay her there. As I gently placed her on the cold metal platform, I thought about how Abraham must have felt when he placed Isaac on the altar. As they began her IV, I suggested that Tiffany tell the doctors the verse she had chosen. With little interest they listened and mumbled something like, "How sweet." As the anesthesia trickled into her body, my eyes locked with hers for one last moment before her glazed eyes rolled back into her head. As she fell asleep, I wondered if I would ever see her alive again.

Five hours later, however, the recovery room nurses wheeled her out on a small gurney and told us to meet in intensive care. As we entered, the frigid temperature caused me to catch my breath, and I squinted as my pupils adjusted to the intense lighting. When I heard a respirator's rhythmic sound to my right, I glanced into a room and felt the sadness of two red-eyed parents as they gingerly held their sick child's hand. My heavy heart became heavier still. I was not prepared to enter the rarified world of a pediatric intensive care unit.

As we approached the curtained cubicle to our left, we found Tiffany bundled under several white hospital blankets. Clear plastic tubes protruded from her head, nose, and arms. My eyes welled up with tears as she awakened and our eyes locked.

Then in a pained, raspy voice she whispered the words of her theme verse: *"Fear not, for I am with you..."* (Isaiah 43:5, NKJV).

As Tiffany spoke those simple words, everyone in the room, our Christian doctor Ben Carson, his two assistants, my wife and I, felt the presence of God. We knew we stood on holy ground. In that place of incredible pain and heartache, the spontaneous words of faith from a five-year-old were indelibly etched on our hearts. Our faith has never been the same.

Tiffany taught me that day that God often wedges crucial faith lessons in the midst of our most painful experiences. I learned that to apprehend the full impact of those lessons, sometimes I must become the student and my child the teacher.

─AUTHOR BIO─

A pastor, Charles Stone is married to Sherryl and has three children. Tiffany is doing well now, more than ten years after her surgery and loves making crafts for others. She also visits the nursing home each week to call their bingo games.

It Couldn't Be

Melissa Sutter

The Happiness. *Me? Pregnant? It couldn't be!* I was thirty-seven years old with two boys who were seven and nine years old. My husband had a vasectomy two years earlier. *Me? Pregnant? Yes!* Disbelief burst into complete happiness. God was blessing us with a larger family.

The Hype. I told my parents the big news and that I was going to wait to tell people since it was so early in my pregnancy. My mom's response was, "That's all right, honey. I'm only going to tell the people I talk to." Her phone was busy for a week! We were all so excited. My husband and I made lists of things we would need and names we liked. Our boys planned what they wanted to teach the new little member of our family. Cards came nearly every day, and phone calls began with "Congratulations" rather than "Hello." October 27, our baby's due date, already held many expectations. Every night our family prayed for our baby to grow strong and healthy.

The Heartbeat. There wasn't one. Eleven and one half weeks into my pregnancy, I heard my doctor say that she was scheduling me for an ultra sound because she could not hear my baby's heartbeat. Within two hours, I was lying down in a darkened room, and my husband and I were looking at our baby on a monitor. Our tiny, little baby was so still. I could not see a heartbeat. "Please, God, breathe life into our baby." No heartbeat. "Please, Father, you raised Lazarus from the dead." No heartbeat. "Please, Jesus, you are the true Healer." No heartbeat. The Creator of this world had other plans for our precious baby. Why?

The Hurt. Our unborn baby had died? It couldn't be! We would never hold our infant? There were no clear answers, and it hurt so much.

The Hope. "If we knew all of the answers, we wouldn't have to trust God," Pastor Daren said. He was right. My hope is in Jesus, and I trust Him. I do not have to know all of the answers because I know the One Who does.

I Wanted

I wanted to sing you a made-up song,
Now you listen to angels' voices all day long.

I wanted to hold you close to my chest,
Now in Jesus' arms you find comfort and rest.

I wanted to spend hours and hours with you reading,
Now you hear stories from the Almighty King.

I wanted to show you how much Jesus means to me,
Now you worship Him on your bended knee.

I wanted to take you to the beach to play in the sand,
Now you go for beautiful walks, holding our Savior's hand.

I wanted to give you special things from our family's past,
Now God hands you treasures that for eternity will last.

I wanted to show you wrong from right,
Now you see no darkness, only the Light.

I wanted to teach you all about the incredible world we live in,
Now you learn from the Teacher, Who made all things on Earth
and in Heaven.

I wanted to give you a home, where you felt safe and secure,
Now you walk streets of gold, where things are perfect and pure.

I wanted to shelter you from pain and sadness,
Now you have complete joy and everlasting happiness.

I wanted to tell you "I love you gobs and heaps plus a ton,"
Now you live with the One who loved you enough to sacrifice
His Son.

I wanted to give you the best of this world by being
a great mother,
Now you have the best and even more by living with
our Holy Father.

─── AUTHOR BIO ───

Melissa Sutter lives in Grant, Michigan with her husband, Mike, and their two children, Chase and Cord. A former high school teacher, she now stays home and teaches her own children. Melissa stays involved with her church and leads a Coffee Break group, a Bible study for women. Reading, writing, four wheeling, and karate are a few of her favorite pastimes.

GOD STILL PERFORMS MIRACLES

Dana Turner

Five years ago I found myself in a very tumultuous storm. This was not a physical storm, characterized by heavy rain and great wind. Instead, this storm was an emotional one, and its symptoms were no less turbulent. My seven and a half year marriage was coming do a disastrous end, resulting in my worst fear becoming reality: I would become a single parent.

My mother raised me alone. She had no outside help whatsoever. Welfare was not an option for her. Instead, she worked fifty to eighty hours per week to support us, so I spent many hours each day alone. I did not want to my children to ever experience anything close to that, but the unhealthy living arrangement we had lived in gave me no good alternative.

Not only would I become a single parent, but also I had no money and no job. I had just given birth to my second daughter, Lauren, and resigned from my company in order to be a stay-at-home mom.

My friend, Sherion, knew of the struggles I had been experiencing up to that point and invited my children and me to live in her home until I was able to figure out what I would do next.

What I needed to take care of first was feeding my newborn baby. Since Lauren was only four months old, baby formula was her only source of nourishment, and this day I had run out, with no money to buy more. I panicked. If I had to be a single parent that was one thing, but I did not want my children to feel the reality of all of these sudden changes. I did not want my children to do without anything. If I had to work hard, I would do it. If I had to do without, I would. But I did not want my children to be negatively affected. They had gone through so much already. I so desired to provide for them and give them some good memories despite our situation, but that evening I could not even give my baby milk.

My heart was aching, and even though my friend Sherion was nearby, I just could not bring myself to share my utter despair with her. I looked in her refrigerator and decided I would give Lauren whole milk, even though her little body was still not prepared for it, but this day there was no milk in sight. My heart sank deeper. Instead of milk, I saw a large pitcher of Kool-Aid. Realizing that this was the only thing I could give my four-month old daughter brought me to tears as I poured the sugary drink into her sterilized bottle.

Lauren drank the juice and went off to sleep. She did not cry or whine or fuss in any way. She just drank the juice and fell asleep. Her peacefulness hurt me more. It was as though she knew that at that time I could not do more for her, and she resigned herself to the reality of it by just going to sleep. I put Lauren and Morgan, my older daughter, into Sherion's bed with her and, afterward, did the only thing that I could do. At midnight I cried out to God for help. I was so sad, angry, ashamed, and so utterly helpless that I just poured out my soul to God. I told Him that if I had to raise my children alone, I would. And if I had to endure some hardship, I would, but I plead for my children. I asked God, in the name of His Son, Jesus, to keep them safe, happy, and healthy, and I asked for food for Lauren. She just could not have Kool-Aid another day. She just couldn't.

The next day I took Morgan to our church for dance practice. As I waited for her class to end, my friend, La Nelle, came to me and said in passing, "Dana, what type of formula do you feed Lauren?" I replied, "Similac with iron." She explained that she has several unused cans of Enfamil formula left over from her young baby, and if I wanted it, I could have it. She said she'd forgotten where she'd bought it but if I could find out, I may be able to exchange them for Similac.

I was so overwhelmed that all I could say was "Yes" and "Thank you." God had miraculously answered my prayer. He heard me when I cried out to Him, and He really answered my prayer. La Nelle gave me eleven cans of powdered Enfamil, so I took them to the grocery store closest to me. I explained to the customer service person that I did not have a receipt, and I was not even sure if the formula came from this store, but if they did and if they would allow it, I would like to exchange them for Similac with iron. After swiping the first can of formula, the representative informed me that not only had the formula come from that store but the brand was more expensive than Similac, so I was able to exchange all of the cans and have several more cans of Similac!

This was the beginning of my trust in God. At that critical time in my life when I had no one to turn to for help, I cried out to God and He heard me and answered my prayer quickly. Since then, He has blessed my life in so many ways. Morgan is still dancing for Jesus at our local church, Victorious Living Fellowship, and was offered a leadership position in the children's church ministry. Lauren is a happy, healthy five-year-old, who will be entering kindergarten in the fall. I have recently graduated from college with my Bachelor of Arts degree in English, and God has blessed me with a wonderful, godly husband. All I can say to all of this is *Praise God!*

Author Bio

Dana Elaine Turner is a wife and a mother of two beautiful, God-loving girls, and an aspiring writer. Her life was completely changed ten years ago when she accepted Jesus Christ as her personal Savior, and this story is just one of the many wonderful things that God has done in her life.

SCAR TISSUE ISSUES

Makisa Upton

I am often amazed at what God uses to open my eyes. I have been saved since I was young and thought that I was basically a good person. Like many Christians, I became hardened to many small sins that had crept into my life. Like most people, though, I was sure that my life was just fine and that I didn't need to change anything and that God should have been glad that I called myself a Christian. God was about to show me differently.

In my junior year of college, I was playing intramural basketball, and my team was doing great. We hadn't lost yet, and our season was almost over. Then it happened. On a fast break, I slipped and completely destroyed my knee. It required a three-hour surgery, and I was on crutches for several months. It was so bad that I was going to have to learn to walk all over again.

I attended six months of rehabilitation, and it was there that God taught me a powerful lesson about scar tissue. I was having trouble getting my knee to bend normally, and my trainer told me that scar tissue was blocking the movement. The scar tissue needed to be broken through so that I could walk again. I had no idea that scar tissue had been building up like this. I could not feel it growing, and quite honestly, I thought I was doing fairly well in my progression. I needed to decide between either forcibly bending my knee to break through the scar tissue or to have a second surgery to remove the scar tissue, resulting in a longer time in rehab and much more pain. I decided to take the shorter route to recovery. I should have run, okay hobbled away when four trainers came walking my way, but what could I do? They each took a hold of my leg and begin forcing it to bend. The pain was excruciating. I had not cried much at all until that day, and then I wept. My trainers kept apologizing and assuring me that it was for my good. I simply sat and cried, and in my mind, I kept asking, "Why me?"

That night when I got home, I was sitting in my room with a huge ice pack for my knee and that still small voice came to me. Scar tissue is like unconfessed sin. It is the stuff that I ignore or refuse to admit I have in my life: pride, lust, selfishness, self-centeredness, laziness, complacency in sharing the truth, and so much more. Like scar tissue, these sins build up in my heart until I am so tied up by sin that I am unable to walk out my Christian life. The most devastating effect of these sin blockages is broken fellowship with the Father. These seemingly little sins that go unconfessed stand between me and God, preventing effective study, prayer, and growth. They become strongholds of Satan, and over time, if they go unattended, they cause hard-heartedness and the once faithful servant falls away. These sins don't come in "guns blazing to take over the heart of a believer," they creep in quietly until one day, I look around, and I am completely entangled in sin.

I came to a point in my heart that I decided I did not care what happened, that I would rather never walk again than go through the pain of rehab every day. I didn't care if I were in a wheel chair or had to use crutches for the rest of my life. It didn't matter to me that I would never ride a bike or a horse, that I would not take moonlight walks with my husband someday or that I would not walk across the stage and accept my diploma when I completed college. I simply wasn't willing to put up with the pain.

One afternoon as my knee was hurting bad enough to make me cry and I was taking pain medicine, I realized that by ignoring the scar tissue I was putting up with pain every day. I was taking medicine to disguise it, but it was there and I knew it. I finally realized that by enduring the pain of breaking through the scar tissue, I could be freed from the every day pain I felt. The trouble was, I was going to need help. I couldn't break up the scar tissue, but my trainers could. It would be painful, but it could be done.

Just like the sin that builds up in my life, I cannot get rid of it myself. I must be painfully honest with God and myself. Confess my sin, repent, and allow God to make real changes in my life. I must go through His surgery on my heart to remove those things and break through the scar tissue, then I can move forward in my walk with Him.

Just for the record, I chose to allow my trainers to painfully break through the scar tissue. I did walk again. I got my diploma with no limp as I joyously walked across the stage. While I am still waiting for that moonlight walk, I am enjoying basketball, volleyball, and walking around the mall during sales. My year-long journey to healing will never be completely through. I still have some pain and some struggles, and there are days when I wake up and have trouble walking, just like in my Christian walk. Just because I break through now, doesn't mean that I won't have this same problem again tomorrow or six months from now. But I know this: if I never give up, I will walk for the rest of my life. In my Christian walk, it is just the same. I will always have sin that comes into my life. How I deal with it is up to me. I pray that I always choose to walk.

————— AUTHOR BIO —————

Makisa Rogers is twenty-four years old and a Graduate of Southwest Baptist University. She has attained a BA in Religious Education and a minor in General Music.

SCAR FACE, THE LILY

Susan Veach

It's a rare genetic skin condition called Tuberous Sclerosis. It began during adolescence, making my face bumpy, angry, and red. From age twelve on, I felt ugly. Boys rejected me, although I later married to prove I was worthy. Even after marriage, I walked looking down. I thought of my skin as an entity separate from myself, an enemy bent on destroying me. I didn't believe in God, but whenever I looked in a mirror, I believed in curses.

So, the name "Susan" means "lily?" *What a joke.*

I never wanted to be a teacher, even though people said I'd make a good one. I knew that job would be a replay of my school years. However, I became a high school English teacher. Looking back, I can see that God closed other employment doors and all but pushed me, kicking and screaming, through the schoolhouse door to my Nineva.

Amazingly enough, and only through God's power, I got along with most of the students and enjoyed them. They seemed to like my classes too, and I easily came to love many of them as the children I couldn't have. A thirteen-year-old student led me to belief in Jesus Christ by witnessing in her journal. Surely that would be enough of a miracle for anyone, but the Lord had more in mind because then, as Job said, "What I feared the most happened."

After ten years in public school, I switched to a private school so that I'd be free to talk about Jesus and pray with students. The sophomores in my new school started calling me "Scar Face." Not when they were in my presence, but I'd hear them outside my classroom door. "What's Scar Face making us do today?" They would ask me to pray for "someone who has scars on their face," and then they'd laugh amongst themselves.

First, I was deeply hurt and angry, and then it occurred to me that I should pray. "Ok, Lord, why am I in this situation? What am I supposed to do?"

You know what it's like when you don't like the answer to prayer? The Lord asked that I talk to the students about what it is like to be different, to tell them exactly how I felt because many of them felt the same for real or imagined reasons. I should expose the vulnerable part of me, showing them that I am not an automaton without feelings, and neither are the other students who receive their taunts. I was to use the Scripture about God looking on the heart and tell them about the disease's destruction in my life. In other words, He was asking me to love the students with all of their sometimes-invisible spots and lesions.

I muttered something about casting pearls before swine. Then God, in His amazing timing, brought about three events. First, in an old literature book in my classroom closet, I just happened to find the story about Scar Face, the disfigured Native American warrior who was transformed by his pursuit of the sun god. The parallel to my life was obvious to me, and I was inspired by the story.

Then a student asked me to proofread her report for religion class. Her subject was a saint from the 1600s who was disfigured with scars from smallpox, yet shortly after her death the scars completely disappeared. There were witnesses. I felt God speaking to me through this story too, reminding me that my flesh is temporary.

The very same week, in another of those weird supernatural events, my dermatologist suddenly offered me the chance to have laser treatments on my face completely free as part of a university-based research project! There were no guarantees that it would work, and it might leave my face in worse shape than ever. *Should I do it?* I thought.

I shared everything with the students and exhorted them to believe that they were not placed here by accident, that each life has purpose, that all things concerning believers are ultimately used for their good. This wasn't me talking; I opened my mouth and the Lord just took over. The students were quiet, but I could see them thinking it over.

After class, one of the boys who had given me the most trouble with classroom disruptions and general ornery behavior stayed behind. "Ms. Veach, I don't think you should have the laser surgery," he said. "I want you to know that we love you the way you are." Then he left, somewhat embarrassed.

If it had been any other student, any of the ones I knew liked me, would I have listened? God, in His infinite mercy, sent me the message in an unmistakable way, through a teenager who spoke completely out of character. Something in me changed and became more lily-like. My God was going to a lot of trouble to convince me.

No, I didn't have the surgery then. Now, three years later, the dermatologist has renewed his offer. Can I say that this time is different because my motivation isn't to look better or ease the old pain? Can I say that I pray my face will serve as research, especially for teenagers who may reach age forty before they encounter the loving God who is completely aware of every lesion?

No. I can't truthfully make those claims as much as you would like to read them, and I would like to write them.

Here's the truth: with or without surgery, I can trust the One who transforms hearts and minds behind the flesh, and who will bring us to the same place, again and again, until the changes are made that only He can see. His Word is the laser that will work my transformation, possibly not during my time on this earth, and make me His lily.

--- AUTHOR BIO ---

Susan Veach has been a high school English teacher for thirteen years. The Lord has used teenagers to bring about changes in her, starting with the ninth-grader who witnessed to her until she accepted Jesus as Savior. She talks to her students honestly about her struggles as a Christian.

TO KNOW ALL OF HIM

Kay Walsh

Lively chatter floated out the window as twelve preteen girls
threw pillows, washed faces, and donned nightshirts for bed. I smiled
as I approached the small four-room cabin where I spent my summers
as a camp counselor while in college. I savored each moment, as this
would be my last summer here. In a few weeks, I would begin my
"real world" job as a middle school teacher.

Suddenly, the chatter stopped. As any camp counselor knows,
quiet can be an indication of impending trouble. With caution,
I flattened myself next to the small cabin and inched closer to the
open window so I could catch the girls at their mischief. They were in
my room, an area off-limits to the campers. Amid muffled giggles and
whispered words, I could tell their prank was harmless. The girls
scampered back to their bunks, jumped in, and pulled up the covers.

Not wanting to disappoint them, I retraced my steps, making
enough noise as to appear newly arriving. The screen door squeaked
as I entered my room. The girls were still. Carefully, I reached to turn
on the light. The light revealed the campers' undergarments hanging
everywhere! They covered the light fixture, the sink, the doorknob,
and my bed. I proclaimed, "Oh! The bra fairy has come!"

Laughing, all the girls crowded into my tiny room, each telling
the story of their personal involvement. When the commotion settled
down, each retrieved her own clothing from my room, hugged me,
and climbed into the creaking bunks. This time the resulting quiet
was a sign of contentment.

The last morning of each weeklong camp was always bittersweet.
The girls scurried to stuff duffel bags with wet, sandy clothes, handmade crafts spouting glitter, and rocks and flowers taken as souvenirs.
A caravan of cars and vans snaked into camp, bringing families to
retrieve their campers. As family members poured out, I smiled and
nodded through introductions. To my amazement, every girl hugged

me and asked for my autograph as though I were famous. Many of them wrote to me long after camp was over.

A deep sense of satisfaction came from the interaction with these campers. To me, this positive rapport confirmed that my calling lay in teaching middle school.

However, my transition from college student and camp counselor to a public school teacher proved to be a difficult adjustment. My personal life, as well as my career, held disappointments.

Living in a new city, I felt far from home. My living situation with five housemates proved to be a stressful contrast to my college roommates. My heart mourned the break up of a long-term dating relationship. My best friend, who lived a four-hour drive away, was diagnosed with a fatal heart condition. Now, the God who had always felt so close, seemed far away.

Prior to this, I never had reason to question God. I lived an ideal life in a happy Christian home. Few obstacles ever stood in the way of my hopes and plans. For the first time, I questioned God asking, "Why?"

One afternoon, just three months after camp had ended, I stood in the empty classroom where I now taught sixth grade. Stunned by an obscene gesture made by a student as she left my room, I hadn't tried to stop her. Nothing had prepared me for the disrespect I encountered during these first days as a teacher. My heart slowly hardened to stone, unable to digest the rebellion of the students and confused by my inability to relate to many of them.

In despair, I dropped in my chair, put my head in my hands, and cried to the Lord, *"Why? I don't understand. Just a few weeks ago girls looked up to me, listened to me, admired me. I was a hero. Why don't I get that respect here?"*

Jesus is the same yesterday, today and forever.

My heart recited the verse I had memorized as a child. What did that have to do with anything?

Jesus is the same yesterday, today and forever.

What did that mean?

Then in my heart, I heard: *They see you differently. You are the teacher.*

I began to understand. In the answering quiet, I realized that as a camp counselor, I was a summer buddy as much as an authority figure. To the campers, I was the cool young adult who was fun, someone who loved to listen to their endless ramblings.

As their teacher, I served as a disciplinarian. Schoolwork became the top priority. At this age, peer pressure had a stronghold on the way students treated teachers.

At this realization, I cried out again to the Lord, "But I am the same person now as I was three months ago! I care about these students just as I did my campers. Can't they see me for who I am?"

In the quiet, my eyes and heart suddenly opened wide. Not only did I see how the students related to me, but also I saw how I related to God.

I had chosen to view only the side of Him I liked. In my mind, He had assumed the role of a 'Disneyland Dad' in everyday life. That's why I couldn't allow Him to co-exist, side by side, with the world where young friends have fatal illnesses, long-term relationships don't turn into marriage, and home seemed far away.

I had to accept that God was not only the One who answers my prayers, giving good things, but also a gentle disciplinarian, teaching me His best ways.

He is Judge, but also Comforter and Redeemer.

He is a refiner, but also provides refuge.

He is Teacher and Friend.

He had not changed just because my viewpoint had changed. I limited Him by my one-sided view of His character. Now, for the first time, I desired Him to be more in my life. I desired to know all of Him. I wanted to know *"Jesus Christ (Who) is the same yesterday and today and forever."* (Hebrew 13:8, NIV)

I looked at my present circumstances and prayed, *Lord, I want to know all of You. Teach me, for I have much to learn. Thank you for trials that cause me to grow, just as a small grain of sand irritates an oyster to produce a pearl. Amen.*

AUTHOR BIO

Kay Walsh lives in Virginia with her wonderful husband, two adorable children, a stubborn horse, and a loveable mutt. She teaches part-time at a university and conducts workshops for teachers.

THIS IS THE DAY

Cathy Welsh-Hulin

It was another anniversary of my late husband's death. Another reminder that his son that he never met would not be raised by him. Painful events ran through my mind again and again. The police coming to my door on a sunny Saturday afternoon to tell me the plane had crashed. Not getting any answers as to why. Just focusing on God being in control. Erik was so young, just twenty-nine. But he loved the Lord, and there was no question as to where his residence was now.

Our son's birth was just six months later. I named him Erik, Jr. after his father. Plenty of family and friends were on hand to support us. My daughter Stephanie was only six at the time of Erik's death. She was home with me the day we were told that the small plane had gone down in the windy hillside of Kerrville, Texas.

On every anniversary of Erik's death I get out our old home videos and watch them with my children in hopes that they would not forget him. Then we look at his photo albums, and marvel at how much his son looked like him when he was young. But when the kids go to bed, I put on the cassette tape of the funeral and listen as his family talked about his short but accomplished life. A graduate of Texas A&M, an aspiring engineer with a great job. A church choir member with hopes to be a deacon. A truly great father, brother, son, friend and husband, as we had carved onto his headstone.

Then the song comes on, sung by his best friend, and my tears can't be sopped by any amount of tissue. Yes, I tell myself, Erik is in heaven with my Savior, my mother, and my brother now. Great company! Wish I were there. But my children need me, so I will pull it together, and trust that the Lord who started a great work in me will complete it!

Sunday morning rolls around; it's the fifth anniversary of that dreaded day. I find it hard again to shake it off. I tell myself, "What if this?" and "What if that?" as I have countless times. Then, suddenly, a song comes into my heart, as if God's trying to tell me something. The song is, "This is the day that the Lord has made, I will rejoice and be glad in it." I talk to God and say, "Yes Lord, I know you made this day, and all my days. But today I'm having a hard time rejoicing and being glad in it."

But as I'm getting ready for church, the song keeps nagging at me, and I keep pushing it back in my mind for fear that the words will form on my lips and I'll forget about Erik and start praising God. That's what the Lord would have me do, sing this song and focus on Him, my Savior, The Lover of My Soul, my Creator, my Father in heaven. I could let Him have this once and for all, right here, right now! A tear forms in my eye as I think of the possibility of letting go of all these years of mourning. I tell myself I'll have to chew on that one for awhile.

As we pull into the church parking lot, I stand staring at the building where my family worships every week, and then some, where my children have all their friends and love attending, where we sing praise and worship to God. *Oh no! I think I can't NOT sing in church! But it won't be a problem, because we won't sing THAT song. It's an old hymn that our contemporary church rarely sings.*

Just as I'm thinking that, still standing outside, a small airplane buzzes by above our heads. Funny, it's just like the ones Erik used to fly, a little Cessna. Even funnier, I'm pretty sure I've never seen one fly around here before, and flying so low, too. There's not an airport for miles. *Weird.* My response is to wave, and a gush of tears comes out of nowhere. It's like I'm waving goodbye to Erik. And I mouth the words, "Good-bye Erik." I tell my son to look up and say, "Let's pray the pilot makes it home safely."

Inside the church, we make it to our usual front row seats, and our call to worship is a new wonderful contemporary re-make of "This is the day that the Lord has made, I will rejoice and celebrate." So I do. I rejoice, I sing the song, I celebrate, I give it all to God on this glorious day. I feel the Lord also rejoicing and celebrating as I grow closer in fellowship with Him.

Now when the anniversary of Erik's death comes around, we try to make it out to his grave and put flowers there out of reverence, but for the most part, we remember him on his birthday instead. We always send a card to his twin brother and enjoy looking at pictures and talking about Erik being in heaven. But the cassette tape and videos are now tucked away tightly in a box, waiting for the day his son will own them, when he's older and ready to know more by the grace of God!

AUTHOR BIO

Cathy Welsh-Hulin is a full-time mom from Dallas. She is re-married and is a part-time journalism student at ACC Community College. She recently started a greeting card ministry at church that keeps her very busy.

BEST-SELLER IN HEAVEN

Russell Williams

When I was a kid growing up in the seventies and early eighties, I'd never heard of Attention Deficit Disorder. If I had grown up in the nineties, I would have been the first kid in line for his fix of Ritalin because of my short attention span. But as I grew older, I learned a skill that helped me concentrate. I noticed that when I was writing, my mind stayed focused. So I rewrote my classroom notes and passages from textbooks until I memorized the material.

Even though this technique worked fine in school, it wasn't helping my spiritual growth. To this day, the preacher still loses me no matter how hard I try to focus on the sermon. Of course, I feel guilty, and I pray that God forgives me for allowing my mind to wander.

However, one day I truly sensed God was saying to me, "Stop apologizing for the gift of imagination and start using it for Me."

God was telling me to take what I viewed as a handicap, and use it as a tool to serve Him. After all, for years, both my wife and my father had been telling me that I should be a writer. So taking the cues from my family and from God, I gave it a shot. And in two and a half years, after reading nineteen books on how to write, and after rewriting my novel five times, I finished my first contemporary Christian fiction manuscript. I'd written a book, and more importantly, I'd written it for God!

Naturally, since I felt God had helped me write this book, I assumed He wanted me to publish it. However, thirty impersonal rejection form letters later, the cruel reality of this world set in, and it looked like this dreamer wouldn't be doing a book tour anytime soon. So why had God led me down this path only to fail to get published? Of course, the rejection has been humbling, and humility is a good Christian trait. But is that the only reason? I don't think so.

As I tap away on my keyboard, writing for God forces me to concentrate on Him, and writing Christian fiction definitely helps my spiritual growth. It forces me to dig into the Bible to make my work Biblically accurate. In fact, the protagonist in my novel has some of the same spiritual flaws I have. Writing my first novel, showing how the protagonist overcomes his spiritual flaws, has been quite therapeutic. God uses writing as a concentration tool for my own spiritual growth!

However, maybe that's not the only reason I write. Isn't there something special about the written word? After all, *"In the beginning was the Word, and the Word was with God, and the Word was God."* I can't say I fully grasp the meaning of John 1:1, but there's definitely something supernatural about words. If that's true, then writing words for God must be a form of worship, much like singing in a church choir. If we must give an account for every careless word we *speak*, then surely our words of worship fixed on paper are also fixed in eternity to our credit, ensuring royalty checks in heaven. And if we entertain angels unaware, then who's to say angels don't sneak a look at our rough drafts and delight in our efforts, even if the writing stinks? Why do we think it's so important to write only for *this* world when the Bible clearly tells us we are not of this world? Who's to say my first novel isn't on heaven's bestseller list right now?

Whether I'm in hardcover, paperback, or heaven's version of an E-book, writing Christian fiction is a great form of worship that leads to spiritual growth. It's God's perfect plan for a daydreaming sheep like me.

— AUTHOR BIO —
Russell Williams is a nightshift Medical Technologist, working for DSI Laboratories in Naples, Florida. He has recently been published in The Christian Communicator, a short story collection called Dreams and Visions, and his first novel, Reborn Again, was released in July of 2003.

THE LITTLE RED WAGON

Sharyn McDonald

We had seen the creative ads in the paper. We'd even driven
past the store and read the brightly colored signs promising unique
merchandise at the "lowest prices in town". Imagine, a discount toy
store, a bargain hunter's dream, a one-stop Christmas shopping oasis
right in our hometown. It was just too much to resist! This place had
it all. Unfortunately, it seemed like every parent in Southern California
had the same idea. The place was total pandemonium. There was no
parking, no shopping carts (they used Radio Flyer Wagons instead),
the noise level was off the scale, and there were kids and red wagons
everywhere!

While I was standing at the counter talking to a sales clerk,
another shopper moved her wagon behind me. When I turned to
leave, I suddenly found myself hurling through the air, flying over
the wagon, and landing hard on the cement floor. Toys were suddenly
forgotten as searing pain shot through my back. Days of agony
followed. Every movement resulted in fresh waves of pain. My
demeanor changed. Usually cheery, I became sullen, discouraged,
and angry. Why had God allowed this to happen? What plan could
he possibly have that included tripping over that ridiculous red
wagon? Didn't he know I had small children to take care of? This
just wasn't fair! I wanted answers!

That Sunday, my husband was scheduled to work and couldn't
take my five-year-old daughter to Sunday School. A friend from
church volunteered to take her for the day so I could rest. When
Darrell got off work, he drove across town to pick her up. On the way
back home, he drove past a man sitting on the curb next to a pair of
crutches. The man was alone, dirty and looked drunk. As my husband
drove by, the Lord spoke to his heart and told him to go back. Not
really understanding why, he turned the car around and went back.

As he extended his hand, the man asked why he had stopped. Darrell simply replied that he had stopped because God had told him to.

Bob, an Eskimo, was a Vietnam vet who had lost both legs in the war. He was estranged from his family, homeless, alone, and his only companion was a bottle of booze. Bob admitted that he needed help, and Darrell knew where to get it. The family that had been watching our daughter was involved with a ministry to men and women addicted to alcohol or drugs.

Without hesitation, my husband helped Bob into the car and drove back to our friend's house. When they arrived, Bob stayed in the car with our daughter while Darrell went inside. When they were alone, my daughter touched Bob's shoulder gently and asked if she could pray for him. Her simple prayer touched his heart. He later told my husband that he had decided he had nothing to live for and had planned to kill himself that afternoon. In what were to be the last moments of his life, my husband stopped, and everything changed in an instant.

Bob listened intently as Darrell shared the message of hope, forgiveness, deliverance, and salvation that comes through faith in Christ. With tears in his eyes, Bob prayed and received Jesus as his Lord and Savior. He began a new life that day. He entered the program and stuck with it. The changes didn't come easily, but each victory was a cause for celebration. He studied the Word fervently and grew in his faith. A year later he returned to Alaska to seek the forgiveness of his family and share the joy he had found in Christ.

God will use whatever method he needs to draw his children to himself. Out of pain, came innumerable blessings. If it had not been for that little red wagon causing my daughter's stay at my friend's house, Bob's life may have ended that day, instead he began an adventure that will last for eternity.

──────── AUTHOR BIO ────────
Sharyn McDonald is a freelance writer living in Garden
Grove, California. She is actively involved in Women's
Ministry and leads a Christian writer's fellowship at
work. She has a heart for ministry and encourages
others in their walk with the Lord through teaching and
inspirational writing. She is married, has three grown
children, and one bright little Penny (her eight-month-
old granddaughter).

GOD'S PERFECT TIMING

Jennifer Bornholm

For the past few years the economy has been struggling to keep its head above water, and everyone has felt the financial hardship it has caused. I was no exception. As a part-time tutor, I was not making enough to sustain myself. I began taking inventory of my bills to try to decide what things were extras that I could do without. One thing I decided to get rid of was my Zephyrhills water cooler. I paid a monthly fee for the cooler, as well as for the five-gallon drums of water delivered every month. I loved having the cooler and water, but with my financial situation, I could not justify paying for it every month.

I called Zephyrhills and told them I could not continue using their service anymore and asked them to come pick up the cooler and unopened drums of water. It was on a cool September morning that the truck came to take it all away.

About two weeks later, I received a letter in the mail from Zephyrhills telling me that they owed me some money for returning the water and cooler early. I couldn't understand why they didn't send the check with the letter, but I was glad to know it was coming because my financial situation had not improved much since discontinuing the water service.

The next few months saw radical changes. I became involved in the middle school ministry at my church, joined the young adult ministry team, and on February 10, 2003, I was baptized. While the most important area of my life, my walk with the Lord, was growing by leaps and bounds, my financial situation was still very precarious. I needed money, but still, that check from Zephyrhills did not come.

In April, I decided to join a group from a different church that visited a nursing home every month. We planned to meet at a bookstore at ten o'clock in the morning and then caravan to the nursing home. I arrived around ten of ten, which was a big deal because I'm not often on time and almost never early. I was the only one there, so I sat at one of the tables outside so I could watch for other members of our little group. Sitting at the table next to me was a girl who seemed very distressed. We began talking, and she told me her story.

Caroline* had come to Orlando from Tampa with her boyfriend for vacation. That morning they argued, and he took the car with her money, driver's license, and credit and debit cards and headed back to Tampa. She had no way of getting home and was very upset. I offered to give her some money so she could take the bus, and she very gratefully accepted. I didn't have the cash on me, so we got in my car to drive to the nearest ATM. While we were in the car I began talking to her about Jesus and asked her if she went to church. She said she was looking for a church but did not join one because she was not yet ready to make that commitment to Christ. She told me her neighbor had given her a bible and said she was going to start reading it. I encouraged her to read it and try different churches until she found one where she could feel the Lord's presence.

When we got back to the bookstore, Caroline asked me for my address so she could send me the money when she got home. I told her I didn't want the money back. The only payment I wanted was for her to start reading her Bible and going to church so she could be convinced of the saving grace of Jesus Christ. Caroline thanked me and walked to the nearby bus stop.

Once everyone from the church arrived, we went to the nursing home. When we finished, I went home and found an envelope from Zephyrhills in my mailbox. It was the refund check! It was a little over the amount I had given to Caroline to take the bus to Tampa.

That experience confirmed three truths about God for me. One, God's timing is always perfect. Now I know why the check didn't come with the initial letter. Two, the Lord rewards us for doing good. I know our ultimate reward is in heaven, but he also rewards us in this life for the good we do. Three, there is no reason to worry about money or other material needs because my heavenly Father knows what I need. After all, Jesus says, "Look at the birds of the air; they do not sow or reap or store away in barns, and yet your heavenly Father feeds them. Are you not much more valuable than they?" (Matthew 6:26, NIV). This verse proves to me that he will provide for all my needs. Our God is truly an awesome God!

*Caroline is used in place of her real name.

─────── AUTHOR BIO ───────

Jennifer is an elementary school teacher in Orlando, FL. She is an active member of Journey Christian Church. She enjoys volunteering for several organizations around central Florida. Jennifer is also an active member of the Chrysalis and Emmaus communities. Her hobbies include cross-stitching, reading, working out, and spending time with family and friends.